being you

being you

A GIRL'S GUIDE TO
mindfulness

CATHARINE HANNAY

PRUFROCK PRESS INC.
WACO, TEXAS

Library of Congress Control Number:2019944864

Copyright ©2019, Prufrock Press Inc.

Edited by Katy McDowall

Cover and layout design by Allegra Denbo

ISBN-13: 978-1-61821-883-4

Printed in the United States of America.

At the time of this book's publication, all facts and figures cited are the most current available. All telephone numbers, addresses, and website URLs are accurate and active. All publications, organizations, websites, and other resources exist as described in the book, and all have been verified. The author and Prufrock Press Inc. make no warranty or guarantee concerning the information and materials given out by organizations or content found at websites, and we are not responsible for any changes that occur after this book's publication. If you find an error, please contact Prufrock Press Inc.

Prufrock Press Inc.
P.O. Box 8813
Waco, TX 76714-8813
Phone: (800) 998-2208
Fax: (800) 240-0333
http://www.prufrock.com

table of contents

acknowledgements

I've been blessed with so much support that adequately expressing my gratitude would take a whole book in and of itself.

The Prufrock team has been a pleasure to work with, especially editor Katy McDowall, designer Allegra Denbo, and publisher Joel McIntosh.

Colleagues in the mindfulness community have helped in countless ways, both in their contributions to the Mindful Teachers website and in making improvements to this book. In particular, I owe a great deal to Christine Fonseca, Sam Himelstein, Jennifer Howd, Deborah Kehoe, Barbara Larrivee, Brandi Lust, Julie Mann, Amiee Peri, Ira Rabois, Pete Reilly, Mary Cay Ricci, Dzung Vo, and Sara Weis.

I've also had tremendous support from my family. My sister, Rev. Deborah Sunoo, helped deepen my understanding of secular and faith-based perspectives on mindfulness and compassion. My niece Alina shared her perspective as a near-peer role model for teen girls. My father, David Hannay, provided essential computer equipment and support. Last but not least, my husband, Eric Peterman, was with me every step of the way, from when I was first thinking through my ideas to when I was making the very last corrections to the final version of the manuscript.

I am deeply grateful to you all.

introduction

You are you! That is truer than true!
There is no one alive who is you-er than you!

—Dr. Seuss

I wish I had a book like this when I was your age. I was so stressed! I spent the whole day worrying about doing something wrong. I had nightmares almost every night. And I had no idea what to do when I felt flooded or overwhelmed by my emotions.

On top of feeling anxious most of the time, I was really confused. It seemed like my parents, teachers, boys, and other girls all had different ideas about how I should behave and even how I should think. It was hard to determine what I really wanted to do and who I really wanted to be.

Do you want to know the worst part? I thought I was the only girl who felt this way.

Now that I'm older, I realize that I definitely wasn't the only girl who felt stressed and confused. In fact, I'm pretty sure that ALL teen girls feel stressed and confused. There's so much to deal with at once:

o   your changing body;
o   pressure to do well in school;
o   expectations from parents and other adults;
o   a social scene full of gossip, frenemies, and bullying;

1

- o   other responsibilities, like a part-time job or taking care of younger siblings; and
- o   serious issues in your family or your community.

When I started learning about mindfulness a few years ago, I thought, "This is so helpful! Why didn't I know about this sooner?" I've talked to several other women who had the same reaction, wishing they'd learned about mindfulness when they were teens.

Mindfulness is for everyone, but it isn't one size fits all. I'll tell you about my favorite activities, but I'm not going to tell you The One and Only Way to practice mindfulness. Instead, my goal is to help you develop a personal mindfulness practice. It's not just about being present; it's about being you.

I've included quotes from girls, ages 15–19, who answered a survey about their favorite ways to practice mindfulness and how it has benefitted them. You'll also hear from my niece Alina, who will turn 20 and start her third year of university a couple of weeks before this book is published.

Plus, there are a lot of different activities. Some of them are traditional types of mindfulness meditation. Others are worksheets to help you connect what you're learning to your own life. I've also included what I do personally, as well as my favorite mindfulness practices from a few of my colleagues.

There are 52 activities, so you could try a different one every week for a whole year. You might want to start a journal of your experiences with the mindfulness activities, especially if you borrowed this book from the library or you're reading the eBook, so that you have a place to write your answers.

Start with Quiz #1: How Much Do I Know About Mindfulness? (see p. 4). Each question relates to a particular chapter, so that will give you a quick way to see what you already know and what you'll learn in this book.

Please read this if you've experienced trauma or are struggling with mental health issues.

If you're dealing with a very serious issue in your life, you could have a strong reaction to certain types of activities. Rather than trying the meditations, body scan, and progressive relaxation on your own, you might benefit from the support of a therapist or a trauma-informed mindfulness teacher.

Please read this if you are a parent, counselor, or teacher.

Here are a few basic tips if you're new to practicing and teaching mindfulness:

1. The quality of your own presence is the most important factor in successfully sharing mindfulness with someone else.
2. Start with activities like five senses, gratitude, and mindful speech. Please establish your own personal practice and seek appropriate training before guiding meditation or progressive relaxation.
3. Please don't push anyone beyond her comfort level. A girl may have very good reasons not to share personal information or not to participate in a certain type of activity, especially in a group setting.

There are many more tips, activities, and resources on teaching mindfulness at http://www.mindfulteachers.org.

how much do i know about mindfulness?

Directions: Circle the answer that shows how much you agree with each statement, from "not at all" (0%) to "definitely" (100%).

1. I understand what mindfulness is and how it can help me.

   not at all   not really   a little bit   sort of   definitely

2. I pay attention to my surroundings and to what I'm eating.

   not at all   not really   a little bit   sort of   definitely

3. I always understand exactly how I'm feeling, and I never get overwhelmed by my emotions.

   not at all   not really   a little bit   sort of   definitely

4. I understand how the brain works and how it can be affected by mindfulness practice.

   not at all   not really   a little bit   sort of   definitely

5. I know several different types of breathing practices for mindfulness or relaxation.

   not at all   not really   a little bit   sort of   definitely

6. I know several different types of body-based practices for mindfulness or relaxation.

   not at all   not really   a little bit   sort of   definitely

7. I never feel stressed when I'm trying to communicate with my friends, family, and teachers.

   not at all   not really   a little bit   sort of   definitely

8. I always find it very easy to treat myself and other people with kindness and compassion.

   not at all   not really   a little bit   sort of   definitely

9. Every day, I express appreciation for the good things in my life.

   not at all   not really   a little bit   sort of   definitely

10. I often share my gifts, advantages, and resources with people in need.

    not at all   not really   a little bit   sort of   definitely

Don't worry if you answered "not really" or "not at all" to most of the questions. That doesn't mean you get a bad score on the quiz. It means you'll probably find this book very useful. You'll have a chance to try this quiz again at the end of the book and see how much your answers have changed.

mindfulness is a practice, not a perfect

You've likely heard about mindfulness, but you might not understand exactly what it means because the word *mindful* is thrown around so much these days.

First of all, you don't have to buy any special clothing or products in order to practice mindfulness. I'm really bothered when I see things like "mindful" snacks, especially when the ads feature skinny models in trendy yoga outfits.

Another misunderstanding is that mindfulness is all about reducing stress. That can be a benefit of practicing, but it's OK if you don't feel relaxed all of the time. Mindfulness can help you to handle your challenges, but it won't make the challenges go away.

The most common misunderstanding occurs because people tend to think that mindfulness is either much harder or much easier than it really is. Keeping your attention focused where you want it to be can be quite challenging. On the other hand, you don't have to be hyper-focused during each and every moment.

Nobody is 100% mindful all day every day. That's why my motto is, "Mindfulness is a practice, not a perfect." Believe me, I could tell you a lot of stories about my less-than-mindful moments!

What Is Mindfulness, Really?

There are actually two different types of attention involved in mindfulness. Single-focus attention means we're "aware of what we are doing while we are doing it." Open-field awareness means "tuning in to the bigger picture even though the main focus of our attention is with what we are actually doing" (Gilbert & Choden, 2014, p. 198).

If you play a sport like soccer or basketball, you use these two types of attention whenever you're dribbling the ball toward the other end of the field or court. Most of your attention is on keeping the ball moving in the right direction. At the same time, you're aware of the boundaries, your teammates and the other team, and maybe people on the sidelines who are cheering you on.

I like to think of it this way:

MINDFULNESS = ATTENTION + INTENTION

Mindfulness is about choosing where and how to focus our attention. Whatever is going on, you're aware of what's going on. Whatever you're feeling, you're aware of how you're feeling. Whatever someone's saying, you're aware of what they're saying.

In other words:

o   What are you focused on right now?
o   Why are you choosing to focus on this instead of on something else?
o   Are you focusing on what's actually happening or on what you want or don't want to happen?

How Do We Practice Mindfulness?

Formal practice, or mindfulness meditation, means setting aside a certain period of time to just be present. There are a few different ways of doing this, which I'll explain in Chapters 3, 5, and 6.

Informal mindfulness practice means paying full attention to whatever is happening right now in this moment. You can do just about anything mindfully, from washing your hair to walking the dog. When Melissa Sutor was growing up, she felt fully present when she spent time with her grandma (as cited in Dawson, V., 2018):

> We'd listen to the crickets and the birds and the wind in the trees, and it was beautiful to just connect with myself, with nature, and with my sister and my grandmother. We were practicing just being. Come to find out, years later—wow!—that's mindfulness. (p. 41)

How Can Mindfulness Help Me?

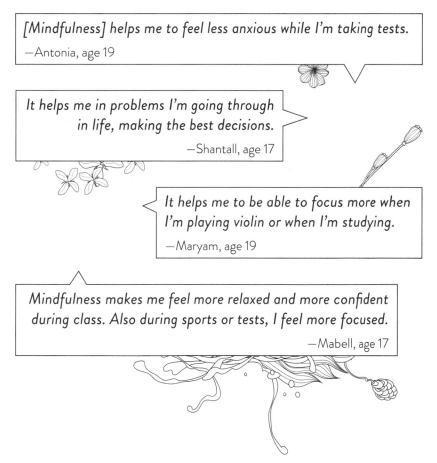

[Mindfulness] helps me to feel less anxious while I'm taking tests.
—Antonia, age 19

It helps me in problems I'm going through in life, making the best decisions.
—Shantall, age 17

It helps me to be able to focus more when I'm playing violin or when I'm studying.
—Maryam, age 19

Mindfulness makes me feel more relaxed and more confident during class. Also during sports or tests, I feel more focused.
—Mabell, age 17

mindfulness is a practice, not a perfect

> *It has helped me with my friends in the sense that I have more patience when I talk to them because there are some days when they really stress me out.*
>
> —Paula, age 17

> *Mindfulness helped me in a lot of ways. When I'm nervous, when I'm sad, when I'm agitated, etc.*
>
> —Arleen, age 15

> *Mindfulness makes miracles, and everyone should be using it.*
>
> —Victoria, age 17

I find that practicing mindfulness helps me feel calmer and more content. But it's important to be realistic. I don't feel cheerful every moment of every day. I still feel angry or sad sometimes. That's a normal part of life.

In my opinion, the most important benefit of mindfulness is that it can help you develop self-awareness. This is different from feeling self-conscious. *Self-awareness* means you have a good sense of who you are and what kind of person you want to be.

Practicing mindfulness doesn't mean you need to change who you are as a person. It can actually help you with all of the things you already like to do:

o   If you're an athlete, a singer, an actor, or a dancer, mindfulness can help you perform better.

o   If you're a writer or an artist, mindfulness can help you produce better work.

o   If you're an activist, mindfulness can help you more effectively work with your allies and maybe even convince other people to join your mission.

There's nothing magical about this. Mindfulness can help you do better on exams because you feel less anxious, but it won't help much if the problem is that you didn't study. The point is that focusing your attention makes you more skillful at whatever you're trying to do:

> When your mind is wandering and you're not truly present, you're much more likely to miss that three-point shot, or forget your lines in the school play, or not solo as beautifully and passionately as you could. (Vo, 2015, p. 179)

You also won't perform as well if you're "worrying about what might happen next, feeling bad about your last performance, or being too afraid to make a mistake" (Vo, 2015, p. 181).

Are you ready to get started? In Chapter 2, you'll have some fun with mindfulness by paying attention to your five senses.

mindfulness is a practice, not a perfect

savoring pleasant moments

Have you experienced anything positive in the past couple of days? Maybe something big happened, like you won a tennis match or you got a really good score on a test. On the other hand, maybe you experienced just a simple little moment, such as hearing a baby giggle at you, playing with a puppy, or seeing a colorful sunset.

My favorite way to practice mindfulness is to really pay attention to what I see, hear, touch, taste, and smell. Because I'm interested in writing and art, focusing on the details of my surroundings helps me express myself more clearly and vividly.

In this chapter, you'll try a lot of different ways to practice awareness of your five senses. You can start with Activity 1: Seven Days With the Five Senses, and then spend more time exploring each of the senses, starting with your sense of sight.

ACTIVITY 1
seven days with the five senses

Directions: In the following chart, write something you see, hear, taste, smell, and touch every day for a week. Or if you like to draw, you can make little sketches instead of writing your answers.

	Sight	Sound	Taste	Smell	Touch
Examples:	*looked at flowers*	*listened to my favorite song*	*sipped a cup of cocoa*	*sniffed pine needles*	*petted my friend's cat*
Monday					
Tuesday					
Wednesday					
Thursday					
Friday					
Saturday					
Sunday					

Note. Adapted from "Noticing the Five Senses: A Daily Mindfulness Log," by C. Hannay, 2014, retrieved from http://www.mindfulteachers.org/2014/12/five-senses-mindfulness-log.html. Copyright 2014 by C. Hannay. Adapted with permission.

Focusing on What You Can See

Most of the time, we don't notice our surroundings because we're lost in our own thoughts or staring at a screen. Here's a simple experiment you can try:

> Close your eyes, take a couple of breaths, and think about the color blue. Blue . . . blue . . . blue. . . . Now open your eyes and look around.

Was the first thing you noticed blue? Or, if there isn't much blue around, did you notice a similar color, like gray or green? Let's try this again:

> Close your eyes, take a couple of breaths, and think about the color red. Red . . . red . . . red. . . . Now open your eyes.

What happened?

If you're like me, everything red just popped out at you. And if there isn't much red in whatever space you're sitting in right now, you likely noticed whatever colors are most similar to red—perhaps orange, pink, or even brown.

Let's try it a third time, with the color yellow:

> Yellow . . . yellow . . . yellow. . . .

What did you notice this time? Depending on what's surrounding you right now, you probably noticed yellow or gold, or maybe cream, white, or pale orange.

It's funny, isn't it? Nothing's changed in the space itself, but it looks different because we've noticed different things. And this doesn't just happen with colors. What you see depends on what you're looking for.

Practicing mindfulness has helped me realize how much my mood affects what I see. If I'm in a good mood walking down the street, I'll notice things like the little flowers growing in the cracks in the sidewalk. If I'm walking down the exact same street but I'm in a bad mood, I'll notice stuff like a piece of trash somebody left on the sidewalk. More often, I won't notice anything at all because I'm so caught up in my own negative thoughts.

I've learned that I can improve my mood by choosing what to focus on. When I'm anxious but make the decision to focus on the good things in my surroundings, I feel more cheerful, or at least calmer. My favorite way to do this is through Activity 2: Rainbow Walk, looking for things that are red, orange, yellow, blue, green, and purple.

I also find it helps me to stay focused when I look at a painting, take a photo, or make a drawing. Activities 3 and 4 have suggestions for these types of mindful art practices.

Focusing on What You Can Hear

Many meditation centers have a bell that rings at different times of day. Every time the meditators hear the bell, they are reminded to bring their attention back to the present moment.

Is there a bell that you hear every day, like a doorbell or a church bell? Or maybe your school has a bell to signal the beginning and ending of class periods? You could also pick a different type of sound to be your mindfulness "bell," like every time you hear an alert on your phone (Vo, 2015).

You can also try Activity 5: Counting Sounds Walk, which will help you stay in the present moment by focusing on your sense of hearing.

Listen to Sounds, Not Noise

Here are a couple of tips if you're distracted by an annoying noise:
1. Try thinking of it not as a noise, but simply as a sound. Take a calming breath and listen, without judging the sound as pleasant or unpleasant (Rabois, 2018a).
2. "Listen as if you had just landed from a foreign planet and didn't know what was making these sounds. . . . Sounds that were annoying become interesting and even amusing when we heard them as some kind of alien music" (Bays, 2011, pp. 49–50).

I have to pause for a moment because I'm laughing at myself. Believe it or not, as I was in the middle of typing that last section, I started feeling annoyed by noise. I guess I'd better take my own advice!

My husband turned on the shower, which is right behind the wall of the room where I'm working right now. That might not sound like a big deal, but I'm more sensitive to noise than most people. I can't focus on reading

ACTIVITY 2
rainbow walk

Directions: Take a walk, and look for something red, orange, yellow, green, blue, and purple. Then start over again at red and keep going through the rainbow. After your walk, write brief descriptions or draw little sketches of some of the things you noticed.

Color	What Did I See on My Rainbow Walk Today?
Red	
Orange	
Yellow	
Green	
Blue	
Purple	

Note. Adapted from "Rainbow Walk: A Mindfulness Activity to Move the Body and Rest the Mind," by C. Hannay, 2014, retrieved from http://www.mindfulteachers.org/2014/10/rainbow-walk-mindfulness-activity.html. Copyright 2014 by C. Hannay. Adapted with permission.

ACTIVITY 3
looking at art mindfully

Directions: It's common these days for people to go to a museum and spend more time taking selfies than actually looking at the art. That's too bad, because art is designed to be contemplated. If we can slow down enough to really focus on what we're looking at, it can feel like we're communicating with the artist, even someone who lived a long time ago.

If you can't get to a museum, there are plenty of other places to find art. You could look at a mural in your neighborhood, a poster at your school, or even out your own window.

1. Examine a painting, photograph, or sculpture.

   Don't just glance at it; really look at it. Try to focus on it for a full minute. If you get bored, try looking at it in different ways. You can shift your gaze slowly from one side of the image to the other. Or you can move closer to and farther away from the image.

2. Your window frames a work of art.

   Look out the nearest window as if it's a painting or photo of a landscape or cityscape. What colors and patterns do you see? How does the image change when you move slightly forward and backward or take half a step to the right or left?

3. Try "mental sketching."

   I like to do this sometimes when I'm stuck waiting around and start to get bored. I pick something to look at, like a tree, and I imagine how I would draw it.

Note. Adapted from "Five Contemplative Art Practices," by C. Hannay, 2016, retrieved from http://www.mindfulteachers.org/2016/08/contemplative-art-practice.html. Copyright 2016 by C. Hannay. Adapted with permission.

ACTIVITY 4
creating art mindfully

Directions: Here are two different ways to practice mindfulness while creating art.

1. Take a mindful photo.

   Rick Heller (2015) teaches mindfulness at Harvard University. He suggested focusing on everyday objects you don't usually pay attention to. When one of his students took a lovely close-up shot of a small yellow flower, someone asked if she was visiting from a part of the world that didn't have dandelions. According to Heller, "Mindful seeing is acting as if you really haven't seen a dandelion before" (p. 153). Heller cautioned that an important part of this practice is to pay attention to your feelings. If you get too caught up in wanting to take a good picture, you won't focus on your present-moment experience of noticing what you're looking at.

2. Do a terrible sketch.

   Of course, it doesn't have to be terrible, but the point is to really focus on what you see, not necessarily to produce a beautiful picture. If you know you're not going to be judged, you can focus more on what you're looking at rather than how other people will react to your picture. (Ironically, this is actually the best way to improve your drawing skills.)

   You can try making a few sketches in the space below or in the blank pages at the end of this book.

Note. Adapted from "Five Contemplative Art Practices," by C. Hannay, 2016, retrieved from http://www.mindfulteachers.org/2016/08/contemplative-art-practice.html. Copyright 2016 by C. Hannay. Adapted with permission.

ACTIVITY 5
counting sounds walk

Directions: Go for a walk and pay attention to all of the different sounds that you hear. When you really start focusing on them, you may be surprised how many sounds are all around you most of the time. For example, on my walk this morning, I heard three different kinds of birds, a buzzing chain saw, and a jogger's sneakers going *fwop, fwop, fwop, fwop* on the pavement.

What sounds did you hear on your walk today?

I heard _____

_____ .

I heard _____

_____ .

I heard _____

_____ .

I heard _____

_____ .

I heard _____

_____ .

I heard _____

_____ .

I heard _____

_____ .

I heard _____

_____ .

Note. Adapted from "Counting Sounds: A Mindful Walking Practice," by C. Hannay, 2015, retrieved from http://www.mindfulteachers.org/2015/03/counting-sounds-mindful-walking-practice.html. Copyright 2015 by C. Hannay. Adapted with permission.

or studying if there's music playing in the background, and any sound at all distracts me when I'm writing.

I'm trying Tip #1 right now: After taking a couple of breaths to calm myself down, I realize that the sound of the shower actually doesn't bother me at all. I was just startled because I wasn't expecting it.

Now I'm trying Tip #2 and imagining aliens dancing at a waterfall. That's making me laugh again, so I'm definitely not annoyed anymore.

Focusing on What You Can Touch

One of my friends had a little baby who was just starting to crawl. They had a great time exploring the floor together because the baby was so excited by the different textures. Wood, carpet. Smooth, rough. Wow!

If there's a baby in your family, you could try "baby touching" together, exploring (carefully and safely) the various surfaces and textures in your house. What do different kinds of cups and plates feel like? How about a teddy bear or another stuffed animal?

Even if you don't have a baby to play with, you can still try "baby touching" on your own. Try touching this book (or the edges of your device, if you're reading the eBook version) as if you've never touched a book before. What does it feel like? How about your chair, desk, or table?

It's amazing how many textures you can find if you look for different things to touch. How about "the petals of flowers, the earth, the fur of a dog or cat" (Gelb, 2004, p. 133)?

Get creative and look for other things you can touch, either around your house or outside in the natural world (see Activity 6: Baby Touch). Just don't do what a couple of my students did. One girl tried petting a squirrel, and it bit her. Another girl didn't realize a pretty little three-leafed plant was actually poison ivy.

Another way to focus on the sense of touch is to shift your attention to your feet. What do the bottoms of your feet feel like when you're walking? How do they feel when you're walking inside or outside, or when you're wearing a different pair of shoes, slippers, or sandals?

I like to focus on the bottoms of my feet when I'm feeling nervous, especially at the dentist. After all, my feet are about as far away as I can get from my teeth!

ACTIVITY 6
baby touch

Directions: Try touching the everyday objects around you as if you're exploring the world for the first time. How many different textures can you find? In the spaces below, write a couple of adjectives that describe how each object feels to you.

Name of Object	How Does It Feel?
Example: Carpet	*flat and rough*
Example: Pencil	*smooth and bumpy*

Note. Adapted from "Four More Ways to Focus on the Five Senses," by C. Hannay, 2019, retrieved from http://www.mindfulteachers.org/2019/05/five-more-five-senses.html. Copyright 2019 by C. Hannay. Adapted with permission.

Focusing on What You Can Smell

I tend not to think about my sense of smell too much, unless there's a very strong odor or I have a cold that plugs up my nose. But it can actually be fun to focus on different types of fragrances and think about what types of feeling or memories they evoke. For me, the smell of pine needles reminds me of summer camp, and the smell of cinnamon reminds me of my Grammy's apple pie.

It can also be interesting to think about why different people like different types of scents. For example, I think my husband's favorite tea smells like rotting mushrooms, and I have to leave the room when he opens a can of tuna. I guess I don't really like strong odors of any kind, which is why I don't wear perfume or hairspray.

Women wear perfume for different reasons. Some of them are trying to attract men, but it may not be as effective as they think. When men were asked to rate different fragrances, the top choices were "baking bread, vanilla, and grilling meat" (Bays, 2011).

I don't think *Eau de Boeuf* or *Parfum de Steak* will ever become popular, but it could be interesting to ask a few guys what types of smells they like or invite them to join you in trying Activity 7: The Sense of Scents. All you have to do is gather a bunch of different foods or substances with pleasant or neutral odors. (I suppose you could also try this with unpleasant odors, but don't invite me to join you!)

Focusing on What You Can Taste

Eating can be a great way to practice awareness of pleasant moments. Have you ever munched a favorite snack while you were reading . . . watching TV . . . checking messages on your phone . . . doing your homework?

How did it taste? Did you even notice?

Most of us tend to take one bite after another without pausing to enjoy the bite that's already in our mouths. It's a lot more satisfying, not to mention healthier, to fully chew one bite before raising the next bite to your mouth. One way of doing this is to set down your fork, spoon, or chopsticks (or sandwich, or taco, or whatever you happen to be eating) between bites. In Activity 8: Mindful or Mindless Treat, you can try eating one bite of food the way you normally do and another bite in a slow and mindful way.

ACTIVITY 7
the sense of scents

Directions: Depending on what you have available, gather several types of food or substances with different fragrances.

Here are a few suggestions:
- perfume, cologne, or scented soap;
- different types of tea or coffee;
- herbs and spices like basil and cinnamon; and
- plants with a strong scent, like pine needles.

After you've gathered several different scents:

1. Close your eyes if that feels comfortable to you.

2. Inhale and exhale through your nose to clear out whatever scents you might have in your nostrils.

3. Select one of your substances. Sniff deeply. For those couple of seconds, try to only focus on the sensation of smell.

4. Think about your reaction to this scent. Do you like it? Does it remind you of something? What thoughts or feelings does it evoke? You can write about your reaction in your journal or in the space below.

Note. Adapted from "Four More Ways to Focus on the Five Senses," by C. Hannay, 2019, retrieved from http://www.mindfulteachers.org/2019/05/five-more-five-senses.html. Copyright 2019 by C. Hannay. Adapted with permission.

ACTIVITY 8
mindful or mindless treat

Directions: For this activity, you'll need two very small servings of a food you enjoy eating. For example, you could try two pieces of your favorite candy, two berries, or two slices of apple.

1. Eat the first little treat in the way you normally would.

2. Then pick up the second treat, put it in your mouth, and chew it ve-e-ry slo-o-wly, paying attention to all of the sensations in your mouth.

3. Did you have a different experience the second time?

4. Write a description of the two treats in the spaces below.

Name of Food: _____

Description of mouthful #1 (eaten normally): _____

_____

_____

_____

_____

_____

Description of mouthful #2 (eaten slowly and mindfully): _____

_____

_____

_____

_____

_____

Note. Adapted from "Four More Ways to Focus on the Five Senses," by C. Hannay, 2019, retrieved from http://www.mindfulteachers.org/2019/05/five-more-five-senses.html. Copyright 2019 by C. Hannay. Adapted with permission.

A couple of girls named Gagana and Kathy tried this type of mindful eating with chocolate-covered berries (as cited in Srinivasan, 2014). Gagana said, "The second time tasted way better than the first" because "when I savored it, I actually tasted the berry after the chocolate melted in my mouth" (p. 48). And Kathy said:

> The second time was a lot better . . . probably because the second time I observed and thought about the berry a lot more. My grandmother savors everything she eats, probably because when she was little and the war was going on, all she had to eat was potato peels. (p. 48)

A similar way to really focus on what you're tasting is to compare three different types of the same food, as explained in Activity 9: A Mindful Taste Test.

Another fun way to practice mindful eating is Activity 10: Five Senses Snack. If you're eating an apple, you don't have to just focus on the way it tastes. You can feel its smooth peel and look at its red, yellow, or green color. You can listen to the crunchy sound it makes when you bite into it, and then smell the tangy sweet scent of the fruit.

I hope the activities in this chapter have helped you enjoy yourself more by focusing your attention on the pleasant sensations you experience every day. In Chapter 3, you'll learn some ways to mindfully handle unpleasant and uncomfortable thoughts and feelings.

ACTIVITY 9
a mindful taste test

Directions: Depending on what type of food you have available, gather several bite-sized treats, like pieces of fruit, candy, nuts, or spoonfuls of jam. In *How to Think Like Leonardo da Vinci*, Michael Gelb (2004) suggested trying three different kinds of the same food. For example, try different kinds of honey, chocolate, mushrooms, apples, grapes, or vanilla ice cream.

You could do this in a couple of different ways:
1. Compare different flavors of food in the same category, such as:
   * pieces of white, milk, and dark chocolate;
   * raspberry, strawberry, and blueberry jam; or
   * types of honey (where I live, we have clover, wildflower, and buckwheat honey, which taste quite different from each other).

2. Or compare the same type of food, but different brands, like:
   * different brands of milk chocolate or dark chocolate, or
   * different brands of strawberry jam.

It could be fun to try this activity with a friend or a member of your family: The person tasting the food could close his or her eyes or put on a blindfold, while the other person prepares the treats. Of course, you should check first that the other person feels comfortable with a blindfold and doesn't have any allergies to the treats you've chosen.

Note. Adapted from "Four More Ways to Focus on the Five Senses," by C. Hannay, 2019, retrieved from http://www.mindfulteachers.org/2019/05/five-more-five-senses.html. Copyright 2019 by C. Hannay. Adapted with permission.

ACTIVITY 10
five senses snack

Directions: Find a snack that you can open, cut, peel, or crunch into, like an apple, a tangerine, or a piece of candy in a wrapper.

What snack did you choose? _____

Describe your "five senses snack" in the following chart.

Sense	Snack: Outside (the peel or package)	Snack: Inside (after opening, cutting, or peeling)
What do you see (color, shape, texture)?		
What do you feel with your fingers . . . on your tongue . . . inside your body?		
What do you hear . . . as you open, cut, or peel . . . as you take a bite . . . as you chew?		
What do you smell . . . before you open, cut, or peel . . . as you open, cut, or peel . . . after you open, cut, or peel?		
What do you taste? Is it bitter, sweet, salty, or sour? Does the taste change as you bite, chew, and swallow?		

Note. Adapted from "Five Senses Snack: A Mindful Eating Chart," by C. Hannay, 2015, retrieved from http://www.mindfulteachers.org/2015/08/five-senses-snack-mindful-eating-chart.html. Copyright 2015 by C. Hannay. Adapted with permission.

stressed, depressed, and quite a mess

I was annoyed when I saw an ad for a mindfulness workshop that was "guaranteed to make you feel happier and more relaxed." Mindfulness is about awareness. It doesn't mean you're always in a particular mood.

In fact, something unexpected happened a few weeks after I started practicing mindfulness. I'd been feeling like, "This is great! Everybody should do this! I feel so much better!" Until suddenly I didn't feel so good anymore.

When I started paying more attention to my thoughts, I realized how much time I spent ruminating (having the same thoughts over and over). It felt like I was constantly stressed out about what was happening, anxious about what was going to happen, or worrying about something that already happened.

When I started paying more attention to my feelings, I realized there were a lot of emotions I was trying to avoid, like anger, frustration, sadness, and embarrassment.

And when I started paying more attention to my interactions with other people, I realized that I wasn't always using mindful speech. I had a tendency to start talking before thinking through what I really wanted to say. I frequently embarrassed myself by doing that. Other times, I really hurt someone's feelings.

That was a challenging time in my life, but I'm glad I went through it. Now I understand how to respond more thoughtfully rather than reacting in a way that might be hurtful to myself or other people.

Handling Negative Thoughts and Strong Feelings

When I was working on a big project, I kept having thoughts like "Oh, no. I'm gonna mess this up!" I was so focused on my negative thoughts that I had difficulty focusing on the project. Because I couldn't concentrate, I felt even more anxious because I was afraid that I wouldn't finish on time. That made it even harder to concentrate, which made me even more anxious. I was caught in a vicious circle, with my mind going around endlessly in the same negative pattern.

What finally helped was simply reminding myself "I'm feeling anxious." Then I started thinking about why I was feeling anxious: I wanted to do a good job. After that, whenever I caught myself feeling anxious about the project, I'd remind myself, "I want to do a good job." That motivated me to get back to work, and once I was actually working on the project, I felt a lot better. That made me feel less anxious, which made it easier to concentrate. The vicious circle of my thoughts turned into a virtuous circle.

Because we can't control things that have already happened or that haven't happened yet (and may never happen), we can feel a lot better if we shift our attention to the present moment. Practicing mindfulness meditation can also help you realize that "you" are not your thoughts, by separating what you're thinking or feeling from who you are as a person. Do you sometimes feel angry or have unkind thoughts? That doesn't mean you're an unkind, angry girl. It means you are a girl who sometimes has unkind thoughts and angry feelings.

Meditation doesn't mean trying to completely clear your mind so you don't have any thoughts. You can't stop your brain from thinking. That's its job. Meditation is more about becoming aware of our thoughts so we can see more clearly what's really going on, like cleaning a window or the windshield on a car. The first type of meditation I ever did was Activity 11: Labeling Thoughts and Feelings. Give it a try and see if it's as helpful for you as it was for me.

ACTIVITY 11
labeling thoughts and feelings

Directions: Set a timer for a short period of time, just a minute or two, and notice what passes through your mind.

1. Sit somewhere quiet where you won't be interrupted for a couple of minutes.

2. Close your eyes if that's comfortable for you.

3. You don't have to focus on anything in particular right now, just notice your thoughts and feelings as they happen.

4. Give your thought or feeling a name or label, like "school thought," "song lyric," "angry feeling," or simply "thought" or "feeling."

5. Let go of that thought or feeling. When a new thought or feeling comes along, give it a name, like "hungry feeling" or "memory."

6. Keep doing this until your timer goes off.

7. Open your eyes (if they were closed) and bring your awareness back to your surroundings.

What did you notice about your thoughts? If you're like me, you probably were surprised by how many thoughts are going through your head one after another. When we practice mindfulness meditation, we're not trying to get rid of our thoughts or judge them as good or bad. We just notice them and let them go. (By the way, labeling thoughts is just one way to meditate. I'll give you more options in Chapters 5 and 6.)

If you find this practice helpful, you can add another minute or two next time, and gradually increase the number of minutes until you're meditating for several minutes every day.

We each have a typical way that we react to uncomfortable thoughts and strong emotions. Most people do something that may make them feel better for a little while, but then makes them feel worse afterward. Maybe they smoke, or eat too much sugar, or yell at somebody who didn't deserve it.

A lot of girls find that practicing mindfulness helps them pause before reacting, so they can figure out healthier ways to respond to strong feelings.

> *Mindfulness has been helping me to control my emotions. For example, when I got angry or felt stress, I used to scream at people, but when I started to practice mindfulness, I started to have more control in these situations. So, instead of screaming, I try to find a solution.*
>
> —Camila, age 16

In her book on mindfulness for athletes, Dr. Amy Saltzman (2018) talked about "having your feelings without your feelings having you" (p. 75). This means that you're aware of what you're feeling but "your feelings don't negatively affect your performance, control your behavior, or have you say or do something that you might regret" (p. 75). When you have strong feelings, try focusing on your breath or your feet on the ground. Then let yourself feel your feelings "without trying to change them, fix them, or get rid of them" (p. 76).

There's a lot of pressure on girls to be sweet and nice and happy, but nobody feels that way all of the time. Activities 12 and 13 will help you acknowledge how you're really feeling. Sad? Frustrated? Angry? Embarrassed? You could even have two different feelings at once, like "smad," which happens "when you are feeling both mad and sad at the same time, or when you get mad because you are so sad, and you don't want to be sad anymore" (Popowitz, 2017, p. 71).

Acknowledging your true feelings doesn't mean you should necessarily act on them or even say them out loud. There's a big difference between feeling like you want to hit someone and telling him you want to hit him. And there's a big difference between that and actually hitting him! (In Chapters 7

ACTIVITY 12
my strong emotions

Directions: Think about times when you've had an intense emotional reaction. How strong was the feeling? How long did it last? I've given a couple of examples from my own life. Can you think of a few examples from your own life?

You can either fill in the chart below or write your answers in your journal.

A Difficult Situation	My Strong Emotions	How Bad Did It Feel? (Number and/ or Description)	What Did I Want to Do When I Had This Feeling?	How Long Did the Feeling Last?
Example: I got a message that I had to pay for breaking something, but I wasn't the one who broke it.	*Angry Frustrated Worried*	*It felt bad, but I could afford to pay the fine, and nothing else would happen. Maybe 5 or 6 out of 10.*	*Yell at someone; cry; I wanted the feeling and the situation to go away.*	*About 15 minutes, until I called and explained, and they said I didn't have to pay the fine.*
Example: My mom was diagnosed with brain cancer.	*Stunned Scared*	*It felt unbearable. Is 11 out of 10 possible?*	*I wanted a hug. Sometimes I just wanted to sleep all day.*	*For her whole illness! But it got easier over time. It wasn't always 10 out of 10; sometimes only 3 or 4 out of 10.*

A Difficult Situation	My Strong Emotions	How Bad Did It Feel? (Number and/ or Description)	What Did I Want to Do When I Had This Feeling?	How Long Did the Feeling Last?

ACTIVITY 13
how do i really feel?

Directions: Think about times when you told someone you were "fine" or "OK" when you actually felt really bad, or when you felt like you *should* feel a different way from how you really felt. I've given a couple of examples from when I was your age. You can add your own examples in the blank spaces on the chart, or you can write about them in your journal.

What Happened	How I "Should" Have Felt	How I Really Felt
Example: One of my friends made jokes about my body because I was flat-chested.	*It's OK. She's just teasing me.*	*Furious. Humiliated.*
Example: My sister got invited to a dance at another school.	*Happy for her.*	*Envious.*

and 8, I'll give you some suggestions for how to respond calmly when you're feeling angry or frustrated.)

Mindfulness and Growth Mindset

In *Nothing You Can't Do!: The Secret Power of Growth Mindsets*, Mary Cay Ricci (2018) explained the difference between a fixed mindset and a growth mindset. A fixed mindset means that "you believe that your abilities cannot improve very much or change, and because of your thinking, you may choose not to participate, not to learn, and just give up." On the other hand, if you have a growth mindset, "you believe that you can get better at and achieve just about anything . . . [if] you are willing to put in the time, the perseverance, and the effort to do it" (pp. 11–12).

Of course, this doesn't mean that anybody can become a famous singer. It does mean that anybody can become a better singer and "have fun singing in a choir or starting a band or auditioning for your school musical" (Ricci, 2018, pp. 5–6).

Dr. Carol Dweck (2006) has done a lot of research on how our mindset can affect us. For example, she asked people what they'd do if they got a C+ on a midterm and their best friend wasn't supportive when they called to talk about it. People with a fixed mindset said things like, "I'd feel worthless and dumb . . . What is there to do?" (p. 8). People with a growth mindset, on the other hand, said things like "I'd start thinking about studying harder (or studying in a different way) for my next test in that class . . . and I'd work things out with my best friend the next time we speak" (p. 9).

I think this idea of growth mindset applies to mindfulness in two ways. First of all, both mindfulness and growth mindset help us to be less judgmental of ourselves and more understanding when we make mistakes.

A few years ago, I interviewed math professor Rachel Levy (2014) about the contributions of women to science, technology, engineering, and mathematics (STEM). Levy said:

> I think it is important for girls to know that it is OK to fail, especially if they are working hard. That may sound strange, but in order to do STEM, you have to be willing to try and fail and try again. It takes a lot of perseverance and sometimes stabbing in the dark and being willing to play in the unknown. (sec. 4, para. 1)

This is also true for writers, artists, and anyone who's trying to create something new. In her book *Make It Mighty Ugly*, Kim Werker (2014) said:

> It's OK that you're struggling, and it's OK that it hurts, and it's OK that you feel defeated or like a fraud sometimes . . . It's just not OK to use that as an excuse not to try. (p. 13)

Having a growth mindset about mindfulness itself is also important. Journalist Manoush Zomorodi (as cited in Paulsen, 2019) said, "I used to think I was the world's worst meditator. But when I heard you're supposed to fail over and over so you can just start again, I was like, Oh, I can do that!" (p. 55).

It's so easy to get distracted. For example, one night at dinner, I told my husband, "I'm sorry. I didn't hear what you just said. I was thinking about this week's guest post."

"Oh, what's it about?" he asked.

I felt pretty embarrassed when I told him, "Mindful listening."

Yes, I run a website about teaching mindfulness, and my mind still likes to wander whenever it gets a chance. This kind of thing happens so often that I joke about how I should start a Mindless Moments podcast.

"Today on Mindless Baking, we'll be discussing what happens when you attempt to make scones without the butter. But haven't we done that episode already?"

"I don't think so," my husband said. "Last time it was the eggs."

A few days ago, I was feeling proud of myself for staying mindful while I was baking cookies. Then I realized I'd forgotten to turn on the oven.

Sometimes you've just gotta laugh at yourself, right?

On the other hand, sometimes we all do things that aren't a laughing matter. Maybe we hurt someone's feelings or we make a big mistake.

It's uncomfortable to feel guilty or embarrassed about something we've done. Instead of trying to push away these negative feelings, we can use them as motivation to avoid making the same kind of mistake again.

Think about something you regret saying or doing, and what you can do differently in the future. You can write about this in your journal or answer the questions in Activity 14: Next Time, I'll Do Better.

Realizing you've made a mistake can feel awkward or maybe even painful. As you're becoming more self-aware, it's important to be very gentle with yourself. Don't beat yourself up about making mistakes. We all say and do things we regret. It's part of being human.

ACTIVITY 14
next time, i'll do better

Directions: Think about something that you feel bad about doing or saying and what you wish you'd done differently. Then answer the following questions in the spaces provided or in your journal.

1. What do I regret doing or saying? _____
   _____
   _____

2. Why do I regret it? _____
   _____
   _____
   _____

3. Why did I do (or say) it? _____
   _____
   _____
   _____

4. What did I learn from this experience? _____
   _____
   _____
   _____

5. What can I do differently the next time I'm in this type of situation? _____
   _____
   _____
   _____

Note. Adapted from "Next Time, I'll Do Better: Recognizing and Learning From Mistakes," by C. Hannay, 2015, retrieved from http://www.mindfulteachers.org/2015/03/next-time-ill-do-better.html. Copyright 2015 by C. Hannay. Adapted with permission.

Elaine Smookler (2019), who teaches at the Centre for Mindfulness Studies in Toronto, used to work for a professional choir. If anybody sang the wrong note during rehearsals, she just raised and lowered her hand while she kept right on singing. "It didn't have to hold you up, or get you down, or be more than a quick flick of the hand." A little mistake didn't have to turn into a "mortifying mess" (p. 30). According to Smookler:

> A mindful approach invites us to notice that . . . being wrong is not in itself a problem. Problems arise when we become determined to push away our errors. In fact, discovering that we are wrong gives us the opportunity to grow—hurray! This is how we learn. (p. 32)

Do you tend to be too hard on yourself? Look at the situations in Activity 15: Am I My Own Best Friend or Worst Frenemy? Which statements seem more like what you say to yourself?

What Does "Everybody" Think of You?

We all tend to worry too much about what everybody thinks of us. Maybe everybody thinks we're fat, ugly, and stupid. On the other hand, maybe everybody thinks we're too skinny, too focused on our own looks, and too smart for our own good. The details are different, but the feeling is the same: awful.

However, "Everybody" is actually a very small number of people. It's not everyone in the entire world, or everyone at school, or even everyone in your own family. What "Everybody" thinks is usually based on a handful of negative comments from a handful of people. Try imagining a new "Everybody" with a much higher opinion of you, by thinking about the people who really like you and all of the times you've been praised or complimented (Beck, 2001).

The Importance of Self-Compassion

I used to be really hard on myself, but I've learned to be a lot gentler. Instead of thinking "I'm so nervous. I'd better calm down or else!" I'll tell myself, "I feel nervous, and that's OK. I'll take a few breaths and maybe do a

ACTIVITY 15
am i my own best friend or worst frenemy?

Directions: Circle the answer that seems most like how you would react in each situation.

Scenario	My Own Worst Frenemy	My Own Best Friend
How would you react if you tripped and fell in the hallway?	I would feel so ashamed that I never want to go back to school. I would keep reminding myself how clumsy I am.	I would feel embarrassed, but mostly I would feel glad I didn't seriously injure myself.
How would you react if you got a low score on a test or you didn't win a competition?	I would feel that I never get anything right.	I would feel disappointed.
How do you usually react when you look in the mirror?	I usually wish I were prettier. I hate my nose. It's impossible to do anything with my hair. Is that another pimple?	I may not look like a supermodel, but I still like myself.
How might you react if you found out that someone you have a crush on isn't attracted to you?	Nobody loves me. I'm such an idiot for even thinking anybody would be attracted to me.	That's too bad, but I bet there's somebody else who's attracted to me. And there are a lot of people who like me and care about me.

If you circled most of the answers in the "My Own Best Friend" column, that means you treat yourself the way you'd treat somebody you care about. If you circled most of the answers in the "My Own Worst Frenemy" column, that means you're awfully hard on yourself. Remember that nobody's perfect, and being a teen can be really challenging. You'll feel a lot better if you talk to yourself in a more loving and supportive way.

couple of stretches so my neck doesn't feel so tense." And instead of thinking I should be a nice person and not feel angry, I'll realize that I need to be by myself for a while because I feel so angry.

Activity 16: How Do I Talk to Myself? will help you practice being more self-compassionate.

Self-compassion means:

> treating yourself the way you would treat a friend who is having a hard time—even if your friend blew it or is feeling inadequate, or is just facing a tough life challenge. . . . Mindfulness asks, "What am I experiencing right now?" Self-compassion asks, "What do I need right now?" (Neff & Germer, 2018, pp. 9, 52)

We may not be able to get exactly what we need, at least not right away, but we still feel better when we think about how to be kind to ourselves. Practicing self-compassion isn't selfish. In fact, self-compassion is the first part of lovingkindness practice. We send good wishes to ourselves before focusing on other people. (I'll explain more about lovingkindness meditation in Chapter 8.)

In this chapter, you learned some different techniques for noticing and accepting your thoughts and feelings. In Chapter 4, you'll learn more about where these thoughts and feelings come from and how mindfulness can positively affect your mind and your brain.

ACTIVITY 16
how do i talk to myself?

Directions: Think about times when your self-talk has been overly critical. Can you think of a more supportive and helpful way to talk to yourself? Write some new ways to talk to yourself in the following chart or in your journal.

Unhelpful Self-Talk	How I Feel	Helpful Self-Talk
Example: I'm gonna mess this up!	Anxious	I want to do a good job.
Example: I hate my hair!	Unattractive	Maybe I can try a new hairstyle.

monkey mind and lizard brain

When you compare the human brain to the brain of an animal, we have a lot of advantages. We're good at planning. We communicate with each other in sophisticated ways. We even create stories and works of art.

On the other hand, there are also some disadvantages to having such a sophisticated and imaginative brain. Unlike animals, we tend to spend a lot of time on unnecessary stress.

If a chipmunk sees a cat, it runs away, but when the danger is over, it's over. The chipmunk doesn't spend the rest of the day thinking about what might have happened if the cat had caught it, or worrying that the cat might catch it tomorrow. Chipmunks are experts at mindfulness because they always live in the present moment.

There's a lot of research that shows how we humans can benefit from practicing mindfulness. For example, a study in Boston, MA, found that the hippocampus, "the brain's memory hub," increases in size with mindfulness training, "similar to the way a muscle grows with repeated exercise" (Mindful, 2018a, p. 12). Another study found that teens who were anxious and depressed "showed significant improvements" after participating in a mindfulness program (Walsh, 2019, p. 13).

There's no standard test to determine how mindful people are. Instead, there are a few different types of measurements, which are quite different from one another.

First of all, psychologists use surveys and interviews, asking the same questions to a lot of people. They use this information to determine what types of mindfulness practices are most beneficial to different individuals under different circumstances.

Secondly, neuroscientists look at images of the brain to see which areas are activated when we do or think about different things. There are a few types of brain scans:

- o an EEG (electroencephalography) measures electrical activity when our neurons send signals to each other,
- o an MRI (magnetic resonance imaging) shows which parts of the brain are active during various types of activities, and
- o an fMRI (functional magnetic resonance imaging) shows how brain activity changes over time.

A third way to measure mindfulness is by testing the level of cortisol in people's saliva. Because cortisol is a stress hormone, there's a lower level of it in our bodies when we feel less anxious. Scientists use this information to see if certain mindfulness practices help people relax. (Yes, our spit changes when we're stressed. Am I the only one who thinks that's a little weird?)

Your Complex Human Brain

The brain has a lot of different sections, and they interact with each other in a variety of ways. I'll explain about just a few parts that are often mentioned in mindfulness research, and I'll keep things as simple as possible.

The biggest part of the brain, the cerebral cortex, includes the parietal lobe, the temporal lobe, the frontal lobe, and the occipital lobe (Rabois, 2016):

- o the parietal lobe helps us know where we are through understanding our physical self, our location in space, and how we move;
- o the temporal lobe, which includes the hippocampus, helps with our five senses, our memory, and our use of language;

o   the frontal lobe, which includes the prefrontal cortex, helps us pay attention, regulate our emotions, and solve problems; and

o   the occipital lobe helps us to see what's around us.

The brain stem connects the rest of the brain to the spinal cord. This is "the most primitive and 'automatic' part of the brain." It's responsible for keeping us alive and functioning in ways that we don't consciously think about, like making sure our hearts keep on beating (Rathbone & Baron, 2015, p. 7).

Above the brain stem is the limbic system. This includes the amygdalas or amygdalae, two pea-sized, almond shaped parts of the brain. (The name *amygdala* comes from the Greek and Latin word for almond.) The amygdalae help with "emotion, memory, and threat perception . . . When our brain becomes overwhelmed with intense emotions . . . our amygdala[s] and other fear centers of the brain are activated" (Fonseca, 2017, pp. 15, 44).

One way to think about the amygdalae is like "our own personal fire alarm, ready to go off whenever we are threatened emotionally or physically" (Popowitz, 2017, p. 15). That's useful when there's an emergency, but it's a problem when the fire alarm doesn't know when to shut itself off. Imagine what it would be like if an alarm were going off all of the time. It would be very hard to concentrate on anything else, and we wouldn't know when we could relax and when we needed to protect ourselves.

Different parts of our brain do different jobs, so they're useful in different situations. Sometimes we need to respond quickly to a threat or danger. At other times, we need to think through a situation and plan the most appropriate response.

We get into trouble when the wrong part of the brain takes over at the wrong time. For example, if a dog is about to attack you, the best thing to do is fight back or run away. It wouldn't help to try to determine what breed of dog it is, remember your favorite movie about a dog, or pull a pencil and a sheet of paper out of your bag and start sketching the dog's big teeth as they're about to bite you.

It also doesn't help to fight back or run away when you're really not in danger. However, if you've been attacked by a dog in the past, you could have a very strong reaction every time you see a dog—even a really sweet golden retriever. You might feel your heart racing just from looking at a picture of a dog, even though you realize the picture isn't going to hurt you.

A common misunderstanding is that each part of our brain does a specific job all by itself. According to psychology professor Dr. Amisha Jha, "all of these parts [of the brain] never work alone. They always work together, but they work in specific ways together," like the way the different parts of the body work together to do a cartwheel (as cited in Boyce, 2018, para. 25). You touch the ground with your hands and feet, but those aren't the only parts of you that are involved in doing a cartwheel. You also need to use a lot of different muscles in a particular order.

A 3-D Model of the Brain

I know it can be hard to picture all of the different parts of the brain and how they relate to each other. You might like to look at the 3-D model at https://www.brainfacts.org/3d-brain. You can click on different sections of the brain and learn about how they're connected to each other and to different parts of the body. The BrainFacts.org website also has lots of articles about current research, so it's a great resource if you have a strong interest in brain science.

Different Ways to Picture the Mind

Have you ever noticed how quickly your mind can jump from one thought to another thought to yet another thought and on and on to more and more thoughts? Zen teachers compare this to a monkey jumping around from tree to tree. When you practice mindful awareness, you calmly observe your thoughts rather than getting caught up in them. It's like you're observing the monkey and noticing its movements, rather than climbing up in the trees to chase after it.

Here are a couple more animal metaphors that can help you understand your mind and your brain.

The Puppy, the Elephant, and the Owl

Australian mindfulness teacher Bobbi Allan (2015) uses the following metaphor when she teaches kids about the brain. The amygdala is like a "guard puppy." It isn't an experienced guard dog, so it doesn't understand when it should bark: "It sometimes barks to warn us about things that aren't really dangerous, like worries or silly thoughts, or it barks simply because we get too excited or too tired" (sec. 1, para. 2).

The hippocampus is like our "memory elephant," which helps us remember information. When the guard puppy starts barking at things that aren't really dangerous, the elephant feels confused and anxious, so it's hard to remember anything (Allan, 2015, sec. 1, para. 3).

The prefrontal cortex is like a "wise owl." The owl part of our brain helps us think clearly. It convinces the guard puppy to stop barking at things that aren't really dangerous. That helps the memory elephant calm down, "open up its listening ears and remember everything it has learned" (Allan, 2015, sec. 1, para. 4–5).

Lizard Brain

A lot of mindfulness teachers talk about the "lizard brain." That's because when humans feel frightened or stressed out, we can react the same way as primitive creatures like reptiles. The lizard brain gets scared even when you really aren't in any danger, and it can make you lash out and do or say things you regret. Fortunately, your lizard brain is just one part of your whole brain. You also have a human brain that can help you "see the situation more clearly and respond in a way that's healthier for you and healthier for the people around you" (Vo, 2015, p. 17).

Rathbone and Baron (2015) gave an example of what can happen when the lizard brain takes over: Amanda thought that her best friend told an embarrassing secret about her. As you can imagine, this made Amanda feel worried and angry. Amanda sent her friend a text. When her friend didn't respond right away, Amanda sent another text. She got more and more anxious when she didn't hear back from her friend, so she kept sending more and more texts, and the tone kept getting angrier and angrier. At the end of the day, she found out that her best friend hadn't actually told her secret, so everything was fine. But Amanda then had a new problem. Her best friend was really hurt and angry about all of the texts accusing her of something she didn't do.

Have you ever experienced something like this? Maybe you were really worried about something that didn't happen, or you got angry and said something you regret? You can write about your experience in your journal or in Activity 17: When Does My Lizard Brain Turn Into Godzilla?

"Remember that creativity is what sets humans apart from lizards" (Werker, 2014, p. 88). Because you're not a reptile, you can use your creative human brain to determine ways to respond more skillfully. You can calm

ACTIVITY 17
when does my lizard brain turn into godzilla?

Directions: Think about a time when you overreacted and what you could have done differently. Then answer the questions in the spaces provided or in your journal.

1. Why was I upset? _____

   _____

   _____

2. How did I overreact? What did I do? _____

   _____

   _____

   _____

3. Were there any signals that my lizard brain was getting out of control? _____

   _____

   _____

   _____

4. Have I noticed these signals before? _____

   _____

   _____

   _____

5. The next time I start to overreact, what can I do to turn my inner Godzilla into a little baby lizard?

   _____

   _____

   _____

   _____

yourself down if you're feeling anxious or angry, or if your monkey mind is jumping around all over the place.

Which of the metaphors do you like the best? Do you sometimes feel like your mind is a monkey, your brain is a lizard, and you really need a wise owl to help you calm down? Maybe you'd prefer to think of a different animal, like a galloping horse when your mind is racing, or a turtle when you feel overwhelmed and just want to hide in your shell. Perhaps your brain isn't like an animal, but more like a machine or a computer or a lake or a forest.

You can write a description or make a sketch in your journal or in Activity 18: How Do I Picture My Mind and My Brain? However you like to imagine it, you've got an amazing brain.

In this chapter, we focused on how your brain works and how mindfulness can help you use your mind more effectively. In Chapter 5, you'll learn more about how stress affects your mind and your body. You'll also learn several breathing techniques that can help you stay calm and do your best while taking exams, playing sports, or giving a performance.

ACTIVITY 18
how do i picture my mind and my brain?

Directions: In the space below or in your journal, write a description or draw a picture of your mind. If you tend to be critical of your own writing or drawing, remember that this is just an exercise. You don't have to show it to anyone else if you don't want to.

What My Mind Looks Like to Me

one breath at a time

No matter where you are or what you're doing, you're always breathing and you always live inside your body. That sounds obvious, doesn't it? But how often do you actually pay attention to your breath or to other physical sensations?

Focusing on breathing is one of the most popular ways to practice present-moment awareness. After all, it's the one thing we're always doing, whether we pay attention to it or not. We don't need to be in a special place or situation in order to breathe.

Different types of breathing practices can also help calm our bodies down when we're feeling anxious or stressed.

How Your Body Responds to Stress

Dr. Dzung Vo (2015), a pediatrician specializing in adolescent medicine, listed many ways your body can react to stress, including:

o   Your heart may feel like it's pounding in your chest.
o   Your breath may get faster or shallower.

o	The muscles in your arms, back, and neck may get tight and tense.

o	Your stomach may feel sick or sore: "Different people experience this in different ways . . . 'That made me want to throw up,' or 'I got butterflies in my stomach.'" (p. 14)

You've probably heard of three typical reactions to something stressful or frightening: fight, flight, or freeze. This doesn't mean we always punch someone or run away. It means our body feels like it wants to do that.

If you're having a fight response, you might clench your hands into fists or your voice might get louder. If you're having a flight response, you might feel trapped and want to get away. And a freeze response makes you feel like you're paralyzed or frozen, so you can't move. Any of these responses might be helpful or unhelpful, depending on the situation.

Have you ever seen a couple of kids start fighting over some little thing? Do you know anybody who skipped class because he was nervous about taking a test? Does one of your friends freeze up when the teacher calls on her and she doesn't know the answer? In those cases, going into fight, flight, or freeze mode probably makes the situation worse.

On the other hand, if you really are in danger, your stress response can help keep you safe. If you hit or push away someone who's attacking you, that's your fight response protecting you. Or let's say you're crossing the street and you see a car coming toward you. Your flight response will help you run as fast as you can to get safely to the other side of the street. Or if you hear gunshots, your freeze response will help you hide and stay still so the shooter won't notice you.

There are also a couple of other beneficial responses to stress. A challenge response is similar to fight-or-flight, but you feel excited instead of afraid. A dancer named Tyna felt a challenge response before her dance recitals (Fonseca, 2017): "She felt 'wired' and super-alert. It wasn't like the stress she felt when she was scared or overwhelmed. This response was energizing. It fueled her and enabled her to give a better performance" (p. 19).

Finally, there's the tend-and-befriend response. When this happens, our bodies respond to stress by activating oxytocin, which "enables our brain to be more socially aware and rewards us for positive social behavior" (Fonseca, 2017, p. 19).

Most of us have a typical reaction every time we're feeling nervous or scared. In my case, I tend to have a flight response, but it depends on the situation. I had an interesting experience several years ago when I went through all five of the different types of stress responses one after another.

Here's what happened: A male friend tried putting his arm around my shoulders, and I completely freaked out because of a bad experience in the past with a different guy. It felt like my body remembered what happened before and acted as if that past experience was happening again.

First, I froze. When my friend asked me what was wrong, I couldn't move or speak. Then, my flight instinct kicked in. I desperately wanted to get away from him, but he kept moving the same direction I was going. That meant he kept getting between me and the door. My fight instinct was activated, and I shoved past him to get out of the room.

In this situation, I wasn't really in any danger. I was with a close friend who treated me like a sister. After I calmed down and thought about it rationally, I realized he was just being friendly and not trying to hurt me.

I felt nervous about talking to my friend after I'd shoved him away. My challenge response gave me the courage to contact him so we could talk about what happened. He was very nice about it, and he didn't blame me for needing to protect myself. We had a tend-and-befriend moment of connection. The next time I saw him, he asked if he could give me a hug. I said, "Yes, please," so he gave me a bear hug.

Can you think of any times when you were helped by your own fight, flight, freeze, challenge, or tend-and-befriend response? You can write about your experiences in your journal or in Activity 19: How Does My Stress Response Help Me?

Breath-Based Practices for Mindfulness or Relaxation

It may not sound exciting to focus on your breath, but it's actually a very popular way to practice mindfulness. Breathing exercises can help if you tend to get really nervous during exams or class presentations. They can also help athletes and performers (actors, dancers, and musicians) stay calm and focused. And they can help you stay level-headed when you're angry, so you don't say or do something you regret.

ACTIVITY 19
how does my stress response help me?

Directions: Think of situations when you were helped by your stress responses: *fight*, *flight*, *freeze*, *challenge*, and *tend and befriend*. Write about your experiences in the space provided or in your journal.

Helpful Stress Response	Example From My Life
Protection From Danger	
Feeling Closer to Others	
Better Performance	
Other Example	

More than half of the girls I surveyed mentioned breathing as their favorite way or one of their favorite ways to practice mindfulness. Here's what a few of them had to say:

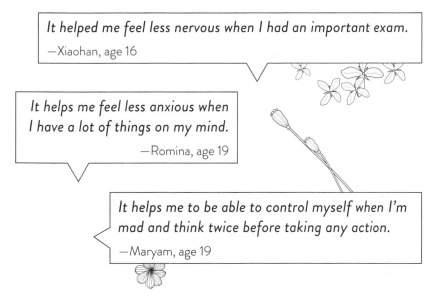

It helped me feel less nervous when I had an important exam.
—Xiaohan, age 16

It helps me feel less anxious when I have a lot of things on my mind.
—Romina, age 19

It helps me to be able to control myself when I'm mad and think twice before taking any action.
—Maryam, age 19

Sometimes you can concentrate on mindful breathing as a way of focusing your attention. Other times, you might want to use breathing exercises to help you calm down when you feel anxious or nervous.

My niece Alina, age 19, is a theater major and a member of her university's improvisational comedy troupe. She told me:

> I'm absolutely out of my mind with nerves before auditions, and on opening night I feel equal parts nervous and excited. I keep calm by breathing, and typically my friends/cast members will all do some sort of calming down/focusing exercise together.

A Gulp of Air Versus Deep Breathing

A lot of people misunderstand the recommendation to "breathe deeply" or "take a deep breath." They take a big gulp of air instead of a slow, gentle inhalation. Let's try a couple of breaths so you can feel the difference.

First, please read this if you have asthma or any other health condition that affects your breathing.

I heard that it might be a problem for girls with asthma to do certain types of breathing exercises, so I checked with Dr. Dzung Vo. He told me:

For asthma, it would depend on if the asthma is well-controlled in that moment or not. If asthma is well-managed, teens with asthma should be able to do anything that any other teen can do. For other health conditions, it could be specific to the individual and the health condition. So maybe the more important thing is to check in with how you are feeling, and check in with your parent/guardian or doctor first. (personal communication, 2019)

As long as it's safe for you to do this, let's try taking two different kinds of breaths and compare how they feel:

1. Quickly take a big gulp of air and blow it out.
2. Now take a long, slow breath in and a long, slow breath out.

When I just tried this, the first breath felt panicky and the second breath felt soothing. That's what happens for most people. According to yoga teacher Sara Weis (2017), our breath tends to be short and shallow when we feel worried, so taking long, slow breaths helps us to feel calm. One way of doing this is to "breathe in and out deeply as if you are an ocean wave washing on the beach" (para. 9).

If you feel ready to try a mindful breathing meditation, you can start by simply observing the breath for one minute. (See Activity 20: One Minute of Mindful Breathing.) This is a lot more challenging than you might think. If you're like most people, your mind will start wandering after just a few seconds. That's OK. Remember, mindfulness is a practice, not a perfect. The point isn't to stop having any thoughts but rather to practice choosing where to focus your attention.

There are also several different types of breathing practices that can help you if you're feeling stressed. Activity 21: Count the Ways to Count

ACTIVITY 20
one minute of mindful breathing

1. **Set a timer for 60 seconds.**

2. **Sit in an upright but comfortable posture.** Most of us spend so much time hunched over our phones and computers that it can be challenging to sit upright. Just do your best, and remember that you're only trying this for one minute.

3. **Close your eyes if that feels comfortable to you.** If you prefer, you can look at a spot on the wall or on the floor in front of you. The idea is to not get distracted by looking around the room or what's going on outside.

4. **Focus on your breathing.** You don't have to breathe in any special way, just notice the breath going in and out, in and out.

5. **When your mind wanders, gently bring your attention back to the breath.** Notice that I said, "when your mind wanders," not "if your mind wanders." It's completely normal for your mind to wander. That happens to all of us.

6. **When the minute is over, open your eyes (if they were closed) and return your attention to your surroundings.** How do you feel? You may feel more relaxed, but it's OK if you don't. This is a mindfulness exercise rather than a relaxation exercise, so the point is to be aware of your breath, not to breathe in a special way or change the way you might be feeling.

You can try the one-minute mindful breathing a few times, choosing a different sensation to focus on each time, including:
- your belly rising and falling;
- the in-breath, or inhalation;
- the out-breath, or exhalation;
- the air blowing through your nostrils onto your upper lip; and/or
- the tiny little pause in between the in-breath and the out-breath.

Now write about your experiences in the spaces provided or in your journal.

1. Was it easy or challenging to focus on your breath? _____

_____

_____

_____

_____

2. How often did your mind wander? _____

_____

_____

_____

_____

3. What did you think about when you got distracted? _____

_____

_____

_____

_____

4. Would you like to try mindful breathing again? _____

_____

_____

_____

_____

5. Did one minute seem like a good amount of time, or would you like to try a shorter or longer mindful breathing practice next time?

_____

_____

_____

_____

_____

Note. Adapted from "Count the Ways to Count the Breath," by C. Hannay, 2019, retrieved from http://www.mindfulteachers.org/2019/05/count-breath.html. Copyright 2019 by C. Hannay. Adapted with permission.

ACTIVITY 21
count the ways to count the breath

Directions: Close your eyes if that's comfortable for you, or focus your gaze gently downward. Most people close their eyes when they meditate because it helps them to avoid distractions. It's fine to keep your eyes open if that's better for you.

Then try one of these different ways of counting the breath.

- Silently say to yourself, "Breathing in, one. Breathing out, one. Breathing in, two. Breathing out, two." Keep counting the breaths as long as you can. When you catch your mind wandering and lose count, gently bring your attention back to the breath and start counting again. "Breathing in, one. Breathing out, one."
- As you breathe in and out, keep repeating the number to yourself: "(inhale) One, one, one. (exhale) One, one, one. (inhale) Two, two, two. (exhale) Two, two, two."
- Count a certain number of breaths over and over. Some people like to count up to five. Others like to count to 10 breaths. You can try it each way, then decide what works best for you.

Note. Adapted from "Count the Ways to Count the Breath," by C. Hannay, 2019, retrieved from http://www.mindfulteachers.org/2019/05/count-breath.html. Copyright 2019 by C. Hannay. Adapted with permission.

the Breath gives you a few options to try. Activity 22: Flower and Bubble Breathing and Activity 23: Breathing Colors were developed by my colleague Christine Fonseca, a former school psychologist who has written several books for teen girls. Finally, Activity 24: Many Ways to Breathe allows you to reflect on the breathing strategies you try.

I know it can be challenging to focus on your breath when you're reading the instructions or trying to remember what to do. There are a lot of meditation apps and websites with guided meditations. My favorites are Dr. Dzung Vo's recordings at http://mindfulnessforteens.com/guided-meditations.

In this chapter, you tried several different breathing practices. In Chapter 6, you'll learn additional ways you can focus on your physical sensations in order to practice mindfulness or relaxation.

ACTIVITY 22
flower and bubble breathing

Directions: Take a slow, deep breath, inhaling through your nose and exhaling through your mouth. Breathe slowly. It should feel like you are smelling a flower when you inhale, and blowing bubbles when you exhale.

Using the flower and bubbles analogy above:
- Smell the flower (inhale) for a count of 3 (1-and-2-and-3).
- Hold it briefly for a count of 4 (1-and-2-and-3-and-4).
- Blow bubbles (exhale) for a count of 5 (1-and-2-and-3-and-4-and-5).

What happened? Did you feel your body's tension begin to release? Did your mind start to settle?

By focusing on your breath, and making certain you are slow and deliberate with each inhalation and exhalation, you are allowing your body to ease into the reality of the present moment.

Note. From *Letting Go: A Girl's Guide to Breaking Free of Stress and Anxiety* (p. 134), by C. Fonseca, 2017, Waco, TX: Prufrock Press. Copyright 2017 by Prufrock Press. Reprinted with permission.

ACTIVITY 23
breathing colors

Directions: Breathing Colors introduces a specific visualization for deep breathing as a way to help you learn how to breathe into your full body.

1. Start by closing your eyes. (If closing your eyes is uncomfortable for you, you can try gazing at something neutral that won't interfere with imagining different colors.)

2. Picture a soothing color. It could be a beautiful ocean blue, or whatever color you associate with being calm.

3. Take a deep breath and inhale the color. Imagine it filling every part of your body.

4. Picture your stress, worries, and anxiety as a color. It could be a muddy, brownish red, or whatever color you associate with anxiety.

5. Exhale and picture the stressful color leaving your body.

6. Repeat until the calm color is the only color you visualize in both inhalation and exhalation.

7. When you feel calm, open your eyes (if closed) and return your awareness to your surroundings.

Note. Adapted from *Letting Go: A Girl's Guide to Breaking Free of Stress and Anxiety* (p. 136), by C. Fonseca, 2017, Waco TX: Prufrock Press. Copyright 2017 by Prufrock Press. Adapted with permission.

ACTIVITY 24
many ways to breathe

Directions: For each type of breathing that you tried, write down a couple of words about how you felt and when/if you might want to try it again.

Type of Breathing	How Did It Feel?	When Might This Be Useful for Me?
One-Minute Mindful Breathing		
Counting the Breath		
Sensations of Breathing ⁑ nostrils ⁑ belly ⁑ in-breath ⁑ out-breath ⁑ pause between breaths		
Flower and Bubble Breathing		
Breathing Colors		

comfortable in your own skin

Getting to know your body can help you stay healthier and improve your performance in challenging situations like taking tests, acting or dancing on stage, or competing in sports.

It may sound silly to get to know your body: "Hello there, body. Nice to meet you." But this really just means that you become more aware of the signals letting you know that you're hungry or full, tired or rested, stressed or relaxed, healthy or sick, and so on. The best way to develop this awareness is through the types of body-based mindfulness practices you'll be learning about in this chapter.

Let's start with Activity 25: Trying on Different Shapes, by my colleague Pete Reilly, a certified Master Somatic Coach and black belt in Aikido, who leads empowerment workshops for women.

ACTIVITY 25
trying on different shapes

Directions: Can the shape of our body affect our mood, emotions, and ability to act? Let's find out by experimenting with a few different body shapes.

1. Start by standing with your feet apart, arms at your sides, with your palms facing in toward your thighs. Take as long as you need to center yourself. (You might want to start with One-Minute Mindful Breathing.)

2. When you feel fully present, bring your attention to your hands. Slowly raise them in front of you while turning your palms upward. Do you notice any changes in how you feel?

3. Go back to your original position. Settle yourself again. Now, round your shoulders forward. Drop your head so your chin is on your chest. How does this shape make you feel? After a few moments, pull your shoulders back while you raise your head to its normal position. Do you notice a difference in how you feel?

4. Let's try another shape: While standing, lift your chin so that your head is thrown back. How do you feel now?

5. Return your chin to its familiar position. How does that feel?

6. You can experiment with other ways of changing your body shape to see if it affects how you feel. Try tightening the muscles around your eyes and staring hard. After a few moments let your eyes soften. Did you feel a change in your mood? How about if you tighten your lips and chin, and then let them soften? How did that feel?

You probably noticed that certain postures made you feel stronger or weaker, calmer or more stressed. You have the power to choose how you sit, stand, and move when you want to feel calmer or stronger.

Note. Adapted from *A Path With Heart: The Inner Journey to Teaching Mastery*, by P. Reilly, 2015, Tompkins Cove, NY: Irimi Horizons. Copyright 2015 by Irimi Horizons. Adapted with permission.

Healthy Body Image for Teen Girls

Having a healthy relationship with your body is important. After all, you're going to live together your whole life, so you'll be a lot happier if you're friends. A study of college students showed that "women who reported greater awareness and who tended to be nonjudgmental and non-reactive—key mindfulness skills—had less body shame, were more attuned to their bodies, and were healthier overall" (Bullock, 2018, para. 3).

There's too much pressure to look like the media images of "perfect" (often edited) images of girls and women. If you're thin, you're "supposed to" be curvier. If you're curvy, you're "supposed to" be thinner. It's not realistic or healthy to compare ourselves to "models who stand six foot two and weight ninety pounds (thirty-five for each breast; twenty for everything else)" (Beck, 2001, p. 97). Susan Ariel Rainbow Kennedy (SARK, 2000) drew a "dieting elephant" to show how absurd it is to be so focused on how much everybody weighs:

> Animals are all sorts of sizes, shapes, and heights. Where is compassion and respect for our differences? Why do we care so much about who's fat and who's not? We don't turn away from hippos because of their size, yet we turn away from fat or big humans. (p. 56)

Serina, age 13, is 5 ft 11 in. and feels like she's "79 feet taller than anyone else" (as cited in Bartolomeo, Furlong, & Handa, 2018). She told *Seventeen* magazine, "I'm different, and I'm finally starting to see that's not a bad thing. There is stuff you can't really change about yourself, and you should appreciate it all. Be yourself and be happy." Sydney, age 19, always felt self-conscious about her weight until she realized "body confidence does not have a size . . . I want young women to realize that self-worth isn't dependent on size, acne, hair length—anything like that. You should never let those things hold you back" (p. 83).

Seventeen-year-old Linette complained, "I am still flat-chested, and that really bothers me" (as cited in Bernstein, 2017, p. 167). At the same time, eighteen-year-old Monica said, "I hate how all the guys just think I am hot and stare at my chest. I feel pressure to live up to always having to look good, yet no one takes my intelligence seriously" (p. 167).

It seems like we're all trying to be something we're not. I used to wish I had curly red hair until my mom told me about a student of hers with exactly the type of hair I wanted. When the student saw a photo of me and my sister, she said to my mom, "I envy your daughters. I always wanted straight blond hair."

We don't need to try to clone ourselves and all look like the same girl or woman. When I was studying in France, one of my friends would say, "Il faut un peu de tout pour faire un monde." It takes a little of everything to make a world. I mean, how boring would it be if we all looked exactly the same?

Food and Mood

One of the ways we can be nicer to our bodies is by paying more attention to what we eat. Sometimes we don't really taste anything because we're so busy and distracted. Other times we may be so hungry we just wolf down our food. And sometimes we might have trouble recognizing when we don't really need food and are eating because we're anxious or have "the munchies."

On a scale of 1 to 5, how hungry are you right now? (See Activity 26: How Hungry Am I?) I just had a snack break, so my hunger level is at about a 1 out of 5, which is how I usually feel after a meal. I spend most of the day at about a 2 range, and I eat something when I get to about a 3. This is quite different from when I was in high school. I would often be at a 3 level of hunger after a meal, and I spent most of the day at a 4 or even a 5. A couple of times I fainted because I wasn't eating enough. I had an eating disturbance, which basically means I didn't quite have an eating disorder but I had a very unhealthy attitude toward food and my body.

Here are some of the typical signs of an eating disorder (Nardo, 2017):

o   hiding food or eating in secret;
o   feeling anxious until you eat a lot of food, even if you're not hungry;
o   never feeling satisfied, even after eating a lot of food;
o   dieting even when extremely thin; and/or
o   alternating between bingeing (eating too much food) and purging (trying to get rid of the food in your body by vomiting or taking laxatives).

If you do any of the things on that list, please talk to a trusted adult who can help you find the support you need. Practicing mindful eating

ACTIVITY 26
how hungry am i?

Directions: Read the statements below, comparing different levels of hunger.

5   I'm starving! I'll eat anything!

4   I can't concentrate on anything else until I eat something.

3   I have physical sensations of hunger. My belly is grumbling or feels empty.

2   I could eat something, but it's not a big deal.

1   I feel completely satisfied. I don't need to eat any more.

0   I'm stuffed. One more bite and I'll start feeling sick to my stomach.

Now circle the answer that corresponds to how your body feels.

How hungry are you right this second?   0   1   2   3   4   5

How do you usually feel after you eat a meal?   0   1   2   3   4   5

How do you usually feel throughout the day?   0   1   2   3   4   5

Based on your answers, do you think you need to make changes to your eating habits? You can write your answer in your journal or in the space provided below.

_____

_____

_____

_____

_____

_____

_____

_____

_____

can be very beneficial for girls with eating disorders, but you might want guidance from a counselor rather than trying these activities on your own. According to therapist Sherri Snyder-Roche (2017), "eating disorders are often a symptom of something much deeper . . . The real issue is not the food nor our weight, but the feeling of being 'not good enough' . . . insecurity, anxiety, and feeling like we don't fit in" (sec. 3, para. 1).

Body-Based Practices for Mindfulness or Relaxation

Meditation has helped on my bad days. When I go to bed and I'm worried about what's coming next and I can't fall asleep, I get frustrated. That's when I start to meditate and it helps me to clear my mind. Sometimes I count [my breath] or I do a body scan. It makes me feel calm and eventually I fall asleep.

—Paola, age 17

In Chapter 5, we explored different ways you can use your breath to pay attention to the present moment or to purposefully develop a feeling of relaxation. You can do the same thing with different types of body-based practices like the body scan (see Activity 27) and progressive relaxation (see Activity 28).

A body scan is a type of meditation where you very slowly move your attention from one end of your body to the other. I prefer to start from my toes and gradually bring my attention up to my head. If it works better for you to do it the other way, that's fine. You can start from your head and gradually move your attention down to your toes.

A lot of people find that a body scan helps them to relax, but it's OK if you don't feel relaxed. The purpose is to notice the sensations in your body, not to feel a particular way. Progressive relaxation is similar to a body scan. The difference is that instead of noticing whatever sensations are already present, you're consciously trying to relax your body.

In this chapter, we focused on your relationship with your own body and how you can become more aware of your inner experience. In Chapters 7 and 8, you'll learn how mindfulness can help in your relationships with other people.

ACTIVITY 27
the body scan

Directions: Very slowly bring your attention from one end of your body to the other, simply noticing whatever sensations you feel.

1. **Find a comfortable spot on the floor where you have enough room to lie down.** You might want to lie down on a yoga mat, an exercise mat, or a towel, and you can put a pillow under your head if that's more comfortable for you. If you'd prefer not to lie down, you can sit in a chair instead.

2. **Close your eyes if that's comfortable for you.**

3. **Bring your attention to your toes.** Do you feel any sensations in your toes? For example, you might feel tingling, or you might feel where your socks touch your skin. Whatever you're feeling, that's fine. Just notice it.

4. **Now bring your attention to your feet.** Do you feel any sensations in your feet? Again, this could be tingling, or your socks touching your skin. Or maybe you feel your heels pressing against the floor. Whatever you're feeling is fine.

5. **Very slowly and gradually bring your attention up the length of your body.**
   - Notice any sensations in your lower legs, then your knees, then your upper legs.
   - Notice any sensations in your belly, then your torso, then your chest.
   - Notice any sensations in your shoulders, then your neck.
   - Notice any sensations in your hands, your lower arms, your elbows, and your upper arms.
   - Notice any sensations in your head and in your face.

After you've slowly scanned through your whole body, open your eyes (if they were closed) and bring your awareness back to your surroundings.

Now write about what you experienced, in the spaces provided or in your journal.

1. How did it feel to focus your attention on your body? _____

_____

_____

_____

2. What types of sensations did you notice? _____

_____

_____

_____

comfortable in your own skin

ACTIVITY 28
progressive relaxation

Directions: Slowly bring your attention to each part of your body. Feel it tense and tighten, then release into a more relaxed position. If you're not sure how to do this, try pressing that part of your body against the floor (for example, your arms) or scrunching it up (for example, your face).

1. **Find a comfortable spot on the floor where you have enough room to lie down.** You might want to lie down on a yoga mat, an exercise mat, or a towel, and you can put a pillow under your head if that's more comfortable for you. If you'd prefer not to lie down, you can sit in a chair instead.

2. **Close your eyes if that's comfortable for you.**

3. **Scrunch up your toes, then release them.**

4. **Now point your feet, then release them.**

5. **Very slowly and gradually tighten and release the muscles up the length of your body.**
   - ∴ Tighten and release the muscles in your lower legs, then your upper legs.
   - ∴ Tighten and release the muscles in your belly.
   - ∴ Tighten and release the muscles in your hands, then your arms.
   - ∴ Tighten and release the muscles in your shoulders, then your neck.
   - ∴ Tighten and release the muscles in your face.

Whenever you're ready, open your eyes (if they were closed) and bring your awareness back to your surroundings.

Now answer the following questions in the spaces provided or in your journal.

1. How did it feel to tighten and release your muscles?_____

   _____

   _____

2. Do you feel more relaxed now than you did a few minutes ago?_____

   _____

   _____

3. How did this feel different from the body scan? _____

   _____

   _____

THINK before you speak
... or text or insta anything

Have you ever said something you regret? I certainly have. I wish I hadn't passed on a rumor about another girl that probably wasn't even true. I also regret the times when I felt nervous and blurted out answers to questions I really didn't want to answer. And I still cringe every time I remember saying something nasty behind a friend's back and then finding out that he'd heard me.

These days, I try to THINK before I speak, so I don't say something that could be harmful to myself or another person:

T: Am I sure that this is True?

H: Is it Helpful for me to say this?

I: Should I say it, or someone else?

N: Is Now a good time to say this?

K: Is it Kind for me to say this?

I have to say that a lot of teen girls don't THINK before they speak. To give just one example, Olivia, age 16, was about to start a presentation when she heard her friend whispering, "Olivia's thighs are so fat" (Wiseman, 2002, p. 84).

Was this True? Helpful? Should "I" (her friend) have said it Now? Was it Kind?

I have no idea whether it was true that Olivia's thighs were fat, or what size thigh counts as "fat," anyway. I am sure that her friend's comment wasn't helpful, and she shouldn't have said it. The timing was horrible because it distracted Olivia right before her presentation, and it definitely wasn't kind.

You can practice THINKing about mindful speech by reading the different scenarios in Activity 29: Do I THINK Before I Speak?

Think About What You Need

> *Mindfulness has helped me A LOT with my relationship with my family. I can show my feelings easier and have better talks with my family.*
>
> —Daniela, age 16

Do you ever feel frustrated in a conversation because the other person keeps reacting the wrong way? Maybe you just need to complain, but your friend keeps giving you advice. Or maybe you just want to explain your point of view, but your teacher accuses you of "talking back." Or maybe you feel upset and want to be alone, but your mom keeps trying to give you a hug.

Here's the thing. Nobody can read your mind, not even your parents or your best friend.

You may find it helpful to think ahead of time about what you want from a particular conversation. It's like "walking into a grocery store with a list instead of browsing through the aisles; you're much more likely to get what you need and leave feeling satisfied" (Headlee, 2017, p. 55).

Of course you don't have to do this every time you say anything to anybody: "Hmmm, I think what I really want when I say 'Good morning' to my math teacher is for him to respond with an appropriate greeting." But if it's

ACTIVITY 29
do i THINK before i speak?

Directions: For each of the following situations, decide whether the person followed the guidelines for mindful speech:

> **T:** Am I sure that this is **True**?
> **H:** Is it **Helpful** for me to say this?
> **I:** Should **I** say it, or someone else?
> **N:** Is **Now** a good time to say this?
> **K:** Is it **Kind** for me to say this?

Mark ✓ for yes, ✗ for no, or ? if you're not sure. There's no score for this quiz. The purpose of this activity isn't to get the correct answer but to reflect on the situations and whether you've witnessed or experienced something similar in your own life.

1. When I walked into class this morning, I saw that Ms. Jenkins dyed her hair a really strange color. I told her, "Your hair looks great!"

   Did I THINK before I spoke? ____ T ____ H ____ I ____ N ____ K

2. As soon as class was over, I said to my friends, "Ms. Jenkins's hair looks terrible, doesn't it?"

   Did I THINK before I spoke? ____ T ____ H ____ I ____ N ____ K

3. People kept telling me about this strange color Ms. Jenkins dyed her hair. When I saw her, I didn't think it looked that bad, so I told her, "Your hair's not as weird as everybody says it is."

   Did I THINK before I spoke? ____ T ____ H ____ I ____ N ____ K

4. I did really well on an exam. I said to my friends, "I got the top score. What did you get?"

   Did I THINK before I spoke? ____ T ____ H ____ I ____ N ____ K

5. One of my friends was bragging about getting a good score on a test, and I didn't want to tell her I failed. I said, "Congratulations!" then started talking about something else.

   Did I THINK before I spoke? ____ T ____ H ____ I ____ N ____ K

6. I saw a couple of kids cheating on a test. I went up to the teacher after class and told him what I'd seen.

   Did I THINK before I spoke? ____ T ____ H ____ I ____ N ____ K

7. I saw a girl looking at her phone during a test. I went up to the teacher after class and told him she was cheating.

   Did I THINK before I spoke?   ____ T   ____ H   ____ I   ____ N   ____ K

8. I saw Maria's boyfriend leaving the movie theater with another girl. I texted Maria that her boyfriend was cheating on her.

   Did I THINK before I spoke?   ____ T   ____ H   ____ I   ____ N   ____ K

9. I saw Maria's boyfriend leaving the movie theater with another girl. I went up to them and said "Hi," and asked, "Where's Maria tonight?"

   Did I THINK before I spoke?   ____ T   ____ H   ____ I   ____ N   ____ K

10. I suspect my older sister might be pregnant. Without asking her, I mention my suspicions to our parents.

    Did I THINK before I spoke?   ____ T   ____ H   ____ I   ____ N   ____ K

11. I suspect my older sister might be pregnant. I ask her if it's true and if there's any way I can help her.

    Did I THINK before I spoke?   ____ T   ____ H   ____ I   ____ N   ____ K

12. My brother did something that made me very angry. I told him, "It's really hard for me to forgive you. I need some time alone before we talk about this."

    Did I THINK before I spoke?   ____ T   ____ H   ____ I   ____ N   ____ K

13. My name is Kanye. I was upset when Taylor won an award because I thought my friend Beyoncé should have won. I interrupted Taylor's speech and told everyone Beyoncé's video was better.

    Did I THINK before I spoke?   ____ T   ____ H   ____ I   ____ N   ____ K

14. My name is Beyoncé. When I won an award later that night, I invited Taylor back onstage to finish her speech.

    Did I THINK before I spoke?   ____ T   ____ H   ____ I   ____ N   ____ K

15. Kanye asked me, "Do you think I'm a jerk?" I told him "Yeah, but I like your music."

    Did I THINK before I spoke?   ____ T   ____ H   ____ I   ____ N   ____ K

Now answer the following questions in the spaces provided or in your journal.

1. In the above situations, how could "I" have chosen to respond differently, and what impact would that have had on other people?

_____

_____

_____

_____

_____

2. Did any of the situations remind you of something from your own life? What happened, and did you and the other people involved THINK before you or they spoke?

_____

_____

_____

_____

_____

3. Has someone ever asked you a question that you really didn't want to answer? How did you react?

_____

_____

_____

_____

_____

4. Believe it or not, someone really told one of the teachers at my school, "Your hair's not as weird as everyone says it is." Have you ever gotten (or given) a "compliment" that really wasn't a compliment? How did you feel afterward?

_____

_____

_____

_____

_____

_____

5. Have you ever caught someone cheating? Did you say anything? Why or why not?

_____

_____

_____

_____

_____

_____

6. In what other situations have you seen someone THINK (or not) before speaking?

_____

_____

_____

_____

_____

_____

Note. Adapted with permission from Hannay 2015e, 2016b. Copyright 2015, 2016 by C. Hannay.

an important conversation, you can avoid a lot of frustration and confusion if both people have the same understanding of what's going on.

Of course, the other person probably won't feel and say and do everything that you'd like. The other person may have his or her own ideas about what he or she wants to express to you, and what he or she would like you to say and do. Even if the conversation doesn't go exactly as you'd planned, think through what you're hoping to get out of the exchange. We often have an unconscious agenda and feel frustrated or disappointed when the other person doesn't do or say what we've imagined.

Reflect on an important or difficult conversation you need to have with someone. What do you hope will happen? Write about it in your journal, or answer the questions in Activity 30: What Kind of Conversation Do I Want?

Are You a Good Listener?

The most important part of mindful speech might actually be knowing when not to talk. Being a good listener is much rarer than you might think, especially now that most people are so distracted by what's happening on their phones.

When your friend's upset or needs someone to confide in, try to give her your full attention. As Father Greg Boyle (2017) said, mindful listening means "Now. Here. This. Listen here and now and only to this person" (p. 84).

Some mindfulness teachers call this type of focused attention deep listening. As Dr. Dzung Vo (2015) explained:

> One thing we all have in common is that we want to feel heard and understood. When you practice deep listening, you listen just to really hear and understand the other person as best you can. You try not to judge what he or she is saying as 'right' or 'wrong.' You try not to interrupt him or her, correct him or her, or attempt to 'fix' his or her problem. You just listen. (p. 154)

Think about what you usually do in a conversation, and answer the questions in Activity 31: Am I a Good Listener?

ACTIVITY 30
what kind of conversation do i want?

Directions: Think about an important or difficult conversation that you need to have with someone, perhaps a teacher or one of your parents. Write answers to the questions in your journal or in the spaces provided.

1. How do you feel about having this conversation? _____

   _____

   _____

   _____

2. What would you like to say to this person? _____

   _____

   _____

   _____

3. What would you like this person to say or not say to you during this conversation?

   _____

   _____

   _____

   _____

4. What would you like this person to do or not do during or after this conversation?

   _____

   _____

   _____

   _____

Remember that the other person may not follow your "script," but it can still help you communicate if you have a clear idea of what you're hoping will happen.

Note. Adapted from "Mindful Speech: What Type of Conversation Do You Want?" by C. Hannay, 2019, retrieved from http://www.mindfulteachers.org/2019/06/mindful-conversation.html. Copyright 2019 by C. Hannay. Adapted with permission.

ACTIVITY 31
am i a good listener?

Directions: Think about what you usually do in a conversation, and circle the answer that seems most appropriate.

1. I *never* *usually* *always* put down my phone when I'm talking to someone.

2. In a conversation, I *never* *usually* *always* completely focus on what the other person is saying.

3. I *never* *usually* *always* show that I'm paying attention through my facial expression and body language.

4. If I disagree with what someone says, I *never* *usually* *always* wait until the other person has finished speaking before telling him or her my own opinion.

5. If I'm confused, I *never* *usually* *always* ask the other person what he or she means rather than making assumptions.

If you answered "usually" or "always" to most of the questions, it sounds like you're a good listener. If you answered "never" to any of the questions, try fully focusing when someone else is speaking to you. I'm sure others will appreciate your attention.

Would you like to change anything about your listening habits? You can write about this in your journal or in the space below.

Mindful Social Media

It's also important to think about what you're sharing online. Before posting something to social media, ask yourself "Do I really need everyone to see this?" Even famous singers and actors are starting to realize that they don't need to post their every thought. Singer Sabrina Carpenter said she feels lucky to have people in her life who remind her to put her phone down and connect face-to-face (as cited in Mosley, 2018).

Actor Rowan Blanchard (as cited in Feldman, 2018) said:

> Part of my self-care was being like, not all of my life has to be public. I realized that I was sharing, sharing, sharing, because that was the culture I was used to, and . . . I realized, oh, actually, it's up to me what I want to say. And that felt like a way of self-care—it's up to me, it's my voice, I can choose how I want to use it. (para. 5)

Keep in mind that social media is designed to be addictive. The media companies make money from collecting and selling information about what people post and look at online. They want you to spend as much time as possible onscreen so they can collect more information and make more money.

Social media changes so quickly that a new app may become really popular by the time you're reading this. As of right now, Snapchat is the most popular social media for teens, and a lot of girls feel pressured to keep up streaks. If you're enjoying it, that's one thing, but it's not worth it if it's stressing you out.

Violet used to put a lot of pressure on herself to maintain her streaks (as cited in Stanley, 2018). She said, "But when I noticed I had streaks going by accident, I realized there isn't really a point to obsessing over them. They can be real conversations instead of a forced event" (p. 69). Stephanie said it's been "a lot more fun" to manage 15 or 20 streaks instead of 80. And Emma had 173(!) going at the same time, so she decided to just stop. She said, "believe it or not, it wasn't hard or huge—it was actually pretty easy. And I'm much more relaxed now" (p. 69).

Journalist Manoush Zomorodi (as cited in Paulsen, 2019) hosts a podcast that focuses on how we interact with technology. She worries that many people crave an unsatisfying type of social connection. She said:

Getting a 'like' or a 'favorite' is like having a piece of candy. It tastes so good! But you're going to be hungry again really soon. So where's the nourishment? Where do you find satisfaction so that you're not swiping, swiping, swiping . . . ? (p. 54)

I know it can be challenging to limit the amount of time you spend online. Do your best to cut back as much as you can. Surveys show that teens who spend less time than average on their devices are happier. Teens who spend more time than average on their screens are more likely to suffer from loneliness, depression, and sleep deprivation (Twenge, 2017).

It's also important to think about the type of content you're looking at and how it makes you feel. There are all kinds of reasons why social media might make you feel bad.

A lot of kids feel hurt when they see photos of their friends having a good time and realize they weren't invited. This is often called fear of missing out (FOMO), but I think it's more a fear of being left out. It's not just that other people are enjoying themselves, but also that they didn't include you.

Another reason you might feel bad is because somebody else seems prettier or sexier than you. In her Beauty Sick column at *Psychology Today*, Dr. Renee Engeln (2018) recommended unfollowing anybody who makes it hard for you to maintain a healthy body image. A study of female college students in Australia showed that viewing Instagram photos of attractive women made the students feel bad about their own bodies. All of the students saw the same images, but some of them saw comments that praised the setting, like a beautiful beach. The others saw comments that praised the appearance of the women in the photos. According to Engeln, "the women who saw the images that included appearance compliments felt even worse about their bodies" (para. 4).

Remember that any photo you see represents about one second of somebody's day. For all you know, other girls envy something about you and your life when they see what you post on social media.

Think Twice Before Sending Photos

As I'm sure you already know, it's become very common for boys to pressure girls into sending sexy or nude photos of themselves. Maybe the boy will send a photo of himself without a shirt on, and he'll tell the girl she should send a shirtless photo of herself in exchange. Or maybe he'll promise to date her or love her if she sends him nudes. If this hasn't happened to you, it's likely happened to a girl you know.

Caroline, who's now 21, wrote an essay for *Seventeen* magazine about what happened during her first year of college (Hogan, 2018). She really regrets texting nude pictures to a guy she liked. She thought he wanted to date her, but he was just collecting photos so he could show them to his friends on the football team. Caroline wants other girls to know:

> The few moments of self-confidence you may get from sending pics are not worth the aftermath . . . My advice? If you've sent pics before, learn to forgive yourself. If you haven't sent photos, don't. (p. 55)

Even if he's a really nice guy, his friends could pressure him into showing them photos of girls. Also, phones get lost or stolen every day. And what happens if a boy shows nude or sexy photos of a girl to his friends or they get posted online? The girl will likely get a bad reputation, while there are no consequences for the boy. That's totally unfair, but it happens all too often.

Caroline said that her friends helped by not judging her (Hogan, 2018), and I think that's fantastic. I've heard about far too many situations where girls slut shame each other. You never really know what's going on in somebody's else's life. The rumors you hear may not be true, or the girl may have been bullied or pressured into doing something she didn't want to do. Try to support other girls instead of tearing each other down.

Be Kind Online

Sabrina Carpenter (as cited in Mosley, 2018) said, "Using the Internet as a place to attack people, or to share negative opinions of someone, has always been a really strange concept to me" (p. 82). She tries not to take negative comments about herself seriously and takes a break from being online if she's feeling upset. You can practice doing this in Activity 32: Mindful Social Media, which was developed by my colleague Ira Rabois.

There are times when it's better to just let things go. Other times, you may need to stand up for yourself or someone else. Unfortunately, online bullying is very common.

ACTIVITY 32
mindful social media: empathy and letting go

Directions: Try this exercise the next time you're on a social media platform and notice yourself getting angry or feeling hurt by someone's post or comment.

1. Close your eyes, take a few breaths, and imagine the person who triggered your feelings. What exactly was said that set you off?

2. Go back to the message and think about what the person meant. What might she have been feeling when she said it? What might she have been thinking? Why might she have said this?

3. Then shift your focus. If you know this person outside of social media, is what you imagine this person meant by her text or tweet consistent with what you experienced with this person in the past? What might have led her to write what she did? If she was angry, imagine the pain she might have been feeling. In your imagination, wish for her a sense of calm or peace, an easing of her pain.

4. Then shift to your breath. Feel what you now feel as you breathe in and out. Feel how your body expands as you inhale—and lets go, relaxes, settles down as you exhale. Maybe feel your shoulders expand, even raise up a little as you inhale. And as you exhale, notice your shoulders drop, let go, and relax. Just sit for a second with that sense of relaxation and letting go.

Note. Adapted from "Mindful Cell Phone Use, for Students and Teachers," by I. Rabois, 2018, retrieved from http://www.mindfulteachers.org/2018/09/mindful-cell-phone-use.html. Copyright 2018 by I. Raobois. Adapted with permission.

It's so easy to make a nasty comment, or to pass on an embarrassing photo or rumor, and it might not feel like it's really hurting anyone. For that reason, I'm not crazy about the expression "in real life." What you do online is part of your life, especially if that's where you spend most of your time and how you do most of your communicating with other people.

In her book *Cringeworthy*, Melissa Dahl (2018) said it's embarrassing but adorable when her grandma comments "Sure do love you, Sweetie" on whatever she posts and "How nice" when her brother adds a Facebook friend (p. 46). You don't have to go that far, but you can be kind online by choosing not to like, comment on, or share posts that are hurtful to other kids. For example:

> You may receive a text with a picture of someone and be told to pass it on. In that moment, you have to choose: Do you want to be an accomplice or break the cycle of bullying? If you don't send the picture or post on, then it won't reach as many people, and it may stop with you. (McAneney, 2016, p. 86)

Activity 33: How Mindful Am I Online? will help you increase your awareness of your social media habits.

This chapter focused on thinking about what messages you're sending to other people, both in person and online. In Chapter 8, we'll continue the discussion of healthy and unhealthy friendships and how you can support other girls.

ACTIVITY 33
how mindful am i online?

Directions: After each statement about social media use, circle "True" (I've done this) or "False" (I haven't done this).

1. I've felt lonely or sad when I've seen photos of an event I wasn't invited to.

   True   False

2. I've sent a photo or text that I later regretted.

   True   False

3. I've spent so much time on social media that I couldn't finish my homework.

   True   False

4. I've looked at my phone instead of talking to the person I'm with in person.

   True   False

5. I've liked or shared a hurtful or bullying message or post.

   True   False

6. Other people have told me I spend too much time looking at my phone.

   True   False

If your answers were mostly "False," you seem to have a very healthy relationship with social media. If your answers were mostly "True," you'd likely benefit from changing your social media habits.

If you're not happy with your social media use, or if it's causing problems for you, what are some ways that you could change your habits? You can write about this in your journal or in the space provided below.

_____

_____

_____

_____

_____

_____

_____

empathy and compassion

I remember being furious about something when I was 5 or 6 years old, and an adult said, "When you're angry, you should take a deep breath and count to 10." That made absolutely no sense to me at the time. I remember thinking, "1-3-4-5-6-7-8-9-10! What?! I'm still angry!" I can see now that I misunderstood how this really works.

The problem isn't the feeling of anger or frustration but the potential hurtfulness of our reactions (to ourselves as well as to others). Have you ever been angry at someone and then felt embarrassed when you realized you'd misread the situation? Or have you been in the opposite position, where someone scolded you for something you didn't do?

I recently got a letter from the library saying I'd damaged a DVD and had to pay $20 to replace it. Because I'd returned the DVD in perfect condition, I calmly read the letter and thought about the best way to resolve the situation.

No, not really.

Here's what actually happened. I stared at the letter for a few seconds, then yelled: "Gadzooks! I feel quite incredulous!" (Or something like that.)

I knew that I needed to call the library, but I was feeling so angry I was afraid I'd say something I'd regret.

Before I picked up the phone, I paused for a few seconds to breathe and slowly count to 10. And yes, it really did work.

Don't get me wrong. It's not like the situation magically resolved itself with no effort. The first person I spoke with kept insisting I'd broken the DVD and was lying so I wouldn't have to pay for it.

But the mindful pause helped me to remember to speak politely and respectfully, even though I was feeling frustrated and upset. The first librarian finally agreed to connect me to the head librarian. After I calmly explained again what happened, he agreed to look into the situation. A couple of hours later I got an e-mail explaining that the DVD was damaged by someone else, and I didn't have to pay the replacement fee.

I was right as a kid that counting to 10 doesn't make the feeling of anger disappear. What I didn't understand is that the point of taking a few breaths is to pause long enough that we can choose a wise response. My favorite way of doing this is through a practice called TAP, which you can learn about in Activity 34.

Several girls I surveyed mentioned that taking a mindful pause has helped in their relationships with friends and family. Here's what a couple of them said:

Mindfulness has helped me a lot to deal with stressful situations and to think before speaking whenever I'm mad. It helped me to stop from saying things I would later regret.
—Linneth, age 16

[Mindfulness] helps me when I'm doing homework but my sister disturbs me. At that time, I always take a deep breath and tell myself, "it's OK," "don't be angry," "be kind," and so on.
—Mengyue, age 17

ACTIVITY 34
TAP

Directions: There are a lot of acronyms for taking a mindful pause, like STOP or PEACE. My favorite is TAP, which I learned from my colleague Dr. Sam Himelstein (2019), the director of the Center for Adolescent Studies.

TAP stands for:

T: Take a Breath
A: Acknowledge
P: Proceed

When you Take a Breath, you pause for a moment before reacting. This can help you avoid doing or saying something you might regret.

When you Acknowledge, you think about what's going on inside you and around you. For example, if you're having an argument, you might recognize that you're feeling angry and frustrated. You might also realize that the other person is feeling the same way.

Now you're ready to Proceed, taking whatever action seems most appropriate. Sometimes you might decide not to act. There are times when not doing or saying anything can be the most helpful action of all.

You can TAP into how you're feeling right now or during any moment of the day.

Take a breath.

Acknowledge however you're feeling. You can write about this in your journal or in the space below.

After you've finished writing, Proceed with whatever seems like the most appropriate action. That could mean talking to someone, dealing with something you need to do, or continuing to read this book.

Bullies and Frenemies

Most of the time, other people really aren't trying to hurt or upset you; they just have their own perspectives and agendas. But what if somebody is being deliberately unkind? As I mentioned in Chapter 7, teens can get awfully mean to each other, especially online.

Here's a list of the common targets for cyberbullying among teens (McAneney, 2016):

o   kids who have physical disabilities or learning disabilities;
o   kids who are openly or suspected of being lesbian, gay, bisexual, transgender, or queer (LGBTQ);
o   kids who have or haven't dated a lot of people;
o   kids who have any characteristic that makes them look different from other teens (this can include height, weight, acne, and wearing glasses or braces).

Carol Dweck (2006) gave a few more reasons why kids are bullied. She said, "It could be for their more timid personality . . . what their background is, or how smart they are. (Sometimes they're not smart enough; sometimes they're too smart.)" (p. 168).

That's a lot of kids! Nearly everybody is either taller or shorter than average, and nearly everyone either has or hasn't been on a lot of dates.

Understanding you're being bullied can be difficult when the bullying is coming from your own friends. In the graphic novel *Smile*, Raina Telgemeier's (2010) friends constantly criticize and make fun of her. She doesn't realize that isn't how real friends treat each other. After she finally breaks away from them, Raina is lonely for a little while, but then she finds a new group of friends who support and appreciate her.

Ira Rabois developed Activity 35: What Does "Friendship" Mean to Me? to help his students think about the qualities of a true friend.

My niece Alina learned about healthy and unhealthy friendships when she was targeted by a group of frenemies in elementary school and middle school. Some days they'd want to hang out with her, and other days they'd tease or ignore her.

Because she knows what it feels like to be excluded, Alina decided to reach out to new girls at her school. She even started teaching herself sign language so she could communicate with the Deaf girls in her gym class. After she finishes college, she's hoping to join a local theater troupe that

ACTIVITY 35
what does "friendship" mean to me?

For kids growing up in today's world, it can be confusing to figure out what a friend is. Were you ever confused about who was truly a friend or what was expected of you as a friend?

Think of any books you've read or movies you've seen that describe a good friendship. What characters come to mind? What makes him or her a friend? How does one friend treat another?

Many use the word *friend* to describe acquaintances, relatives, and people they hardly know, as well as those they spend time with daily, or want to spend time with daily. They might brag about the numbers of "friends" they have on Facebook or other social media platforms, and keep track of many people. But do they really know any of them? They don't want to miss out. But what are they really missing?

Although you might follow a friend's life on a social media screen, a true friend is someone who ultimately pulls you from that screen.

What is most important to you? Is it how many friends you have on social media? Or the quality or depth of the friendship? What happens if you focus on numbers, or on choosing friends because of what others might think of them, not on what you truly feel?

I think this is how people get lost. They focus on numbers, not quality; on how the friendship appears to others, not on what actually goes on inside their mind and heart. They lose a sense of who they truly are.

The more you are aware of your feelings, thoughts, and motivations, and aware of the other person as an independent, feeling person with his or her own wants and ways of looking at the world, the more likely you will be able to form a lasting friendship.

Note. Adapted from "Befriending Yourself and Creating a Mindful Learning Community," by I. Rabois, 2019, retrieved from http://www.mindfulteachers.org/2019/03/befriending.html. Copyright 2019 by I. Rabois. Adapted with permission.

Alina's Story

I was about 7 years old (second grade) when I first remember being bullied. I remember one day I was on the playground and approached a couple girls. They made several excuses for why they didn't want to play with me.

First, they said that I was too tall. After I pointed out that they weren't the same height either and it didn't make sense, they said they couldn't play with me because I didn't belong to their country club. I don't remember my exact response to this, but I think (hope) it was along the lines of "so what?"

But when they finally told me that I just wasn't fun to play with, I walked away. It feels horrible, especially when you thought that those bullies were your friends. That was the worst part, I think—my bullies weren't mean 100% of the time, which was very confusing.

I think that one reason was that I was not as wealthy as them, meaning that I was not in their country club or neighborhood. However, I think that the main reason was because they felt special being a part of a group, which was made more special by excluding certain people.

My parents' support made a huge difference. I would say tell someone (parents, teachers, a friend) because if you are bullied the worst part is feeling like you're alone. (personal communication, 2019)

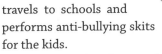

travels to schools and performs anti-bullying skits for the kids.

Alina thinks she was likely targeted at least partly because her frenemies were all White, and her father is Korean American. She said, "I think that people are targeted for anything that makes them different. But as Ben Platt (one of my favorite Broadway actors) says 'the things that make you strange are the things that make you powerful'" (personal communication, 2019). These days, Alina's friends in her college theater program are envious that she looks ethnically ambiguous because it allows her to play a wide range of roles.

The truth is, almost all of us have felt like we didn't fit in at one time or another. There's a famous story that Taylor Swift was teased as a young teen because she liked to write song lyrics. I'm sure she's happy now that she was different from the other girls at her school.

How to Be an Upstander, Not a Bystander

Sometimes other kids will join in the bullying, or won't stand up to the bully, because they're afraid of being targeted themselves. I know that coming to another kid's defense might make you feel nervous, or even scared. You may not be able to stop the bullying, but you can be an ally. You can go up to someone quietly afterwards and ask if he or she is OK. As Alina said, "The worst part is feeling like you're alone." Kids who are getting bullied will feel a lot better about themselves if they know someone cares.

In *Mindset*, Dweck (2006) explained why it's so important to support victims of bullying:

> Victims say that when they're taunted and demeaned and no one comes to their defense, they start to believe they deserve it. They start to judge themselves and to feel that they are inferior. Bullies judge. Victims take it in. Sometimes it remains inside and can lead to depression and suicide. Sometimes it explodes into violence. (p. 172)

Activity 36: How Can I Be an Upstander? is designed to help you to reflect on ways you can support victims of bullying.

Compassion and Lovingkindness

Lovingkindness meditation means sending positive thoughts or good wishes to yourself and other people. Here's a typical way of doing this type of meditation.

First, you send compassion to yourself, using phrases like this:

May I be happy. May I be well. May I be free from harm.

ACTIVITY 36
how can i be an upstander?

Directions: Think about the kids in your school or neighborhood who might be the targets of bullying. Then answer the questions in the spaces provided or in your journal.

1. Do you know any kids who are getting bullied or you think might be getting bullied?

_____

_____

_____

_____

_____

_____

2. What do you think might happen if you try talking to the bullies and asking them to stop? Would it likely help or make the situation worse?

_____

_____

_____

_____

_____

_____

3. What are some additional ways you could support the victims of bullying?

_____

_____

_____

_____

_____

_____

4. What is one small thing you could do this week to help support someone who's being bullied?

_____

_____

_____

_____

_____

_____

Now comes the hardest but most important part: Actually go and do the one small thing you just wrote down.

Did you do that? What happened? How do you feel?

_____

_____

_____

_____

_____

_____

_____

_____

_____

_____

_____

_____

_____

Then you think of someone you love, and send him or her good wishes:

May you be happy. May you be well. May you be free from harm.

Then you picture someone neutral, someone you don't have strong feelings about. This could be a neighbor or a classmate you don't know very well:

May you be happy. May you be well. May you be free from harm.

Then you focus on someone you're angry with or you don't like very much:

May you be happy. May you be well. May you be free from harm.

Finally, you send good wishes to everyone you know, or even everyone in the whole world. You might think about a circle of compassion getting bigger and bigger until there's no one left outside of the circle. You could even include other living creatures in your circle of compassion:

May you be happy. May you be well. May you be free from harm.

Every day, you can choose the same people or different people to focus on. Today I'm wishing lovingkindness to the following people (and critters):
o   myself;
o   my sister;
o   the lady who used to cut my hair, who retired recently;
o   someone I feel a bit frustrated with because she didn't do something she promised to do;
o   the raccoon family that lives in the oak tree in the backyard; and
o   people all over the world, especially teen girls.

This type of meditation may seem easy when you're just reading about it, but it can actually be quite challenging. It could be really hard to send good wishes to someone you don't like. On the other hand, it might be hardest to send good wishes to yourself if you're feeling depressed or you regret something you've said or done. When I'm feeling that way, I remember a Swedish proverb that says, "Love me when I least deserve it, for that is when I need it most."

How to Phrase Lovingkindness Meditation

There are compassion-based practices in every religious tradition. However, the phrasing of lovingkindness meditation in mindfulness classes tends to be adapted from Buddhist teachings on *metta*. This is a Pali word that can be translated as lovingkindness, benevolence, or friendliness (Heller, 2015). (Pali is a classical language from India, related to Sanskrit.)

Secular meditation teacher Rick Heller (2015) developed the following phrasing for his non-Buddhist students: "I'd like you to be safe. I'd like you to be healthy. I'd like you to be happy. I'd like you to be at ease in the world" (p. 13).

According to Dr. Kristin Neff and Dr. Christopher Germer (2018), well-known experts on self-compassion, you don't have to use someone else's phrasing of lovingkindness meditation if it doesn't feel natural to you. Instead, you can use three or four phrases that express what you'd like to focus on. For example, you could say: "May I begin to be kind to myself, May I know that I belong, May I live in peace" (p. 72). Then you can send those same wishes to the other people on your list.

If you're Christian, Jewish, or Muslim, you might prefer to think of God blessing you and all of the people on your list. My sister, Rev. Deborah Sunoo (a.k.a. Pastor Deb), likes to use phrases like "The Lord bless you and keep you," or "May the peace of Christ be with you."

You may also want to do a mini lovingkindness practice throughout the day. That's what I do whenever I catch myself feeling angry or unloving toward someone, or when I see a situation where someone is suffering. Often, I'll use the phrase "I wish you peace" to silently send good wishes to myself and to the other person. Recently I've started using just one word: "peace," or "love," or even "hug!" as a very quick reminder to show myself or someone else compassion and kindness in a difficult moment.

You can practice lovingkindness meditation in Activity 37.

ACTIVITY 37
lovingkindness meditation

Directions: Set aside a few minutes to send good wishes to yourself and other people. You might want to start with a minute or two of your favorite mindful breathing practice.

Choose your preferred phrasing: Buddhist, secular, faith-based, "I wish you peace," or whatever phrasing feels natural to you and helps you feel a sense of kindness or friendliness. Whichever words you choose, say them slowly so the feeling can really sink in: "There's no rush—saying the most phrases in the shortest time doesn't win the race!" (Neff & Germer, 2018, p. 70). It's OK if you don't feel warm and fuzzy, especially when you're sending good wishes toward someone you don't like or you feel angry toward. The purpose is to practice being compassionate toward other people, not to force yourself to feel a particular way.

1. Start by focusing on yourself. Silently repeat the phrases you've chosen.

2. Next, send good wishes to a person you feel positively toward, perhaps a friend or a member of your family.

3. After that, send good wishes to a person you feel neutral toward, perhaps a classmate or acquaintance.

4. Now do your best to send good wishes to a person you feel annoyed with or it's hard to share lovingkindness with.

5. Finally, send good wishes to a large group of people, and maybe even to the whole world.

As with other types of meditation, you may find it easier to listen to a recording rather than reading and remembering the instructions. As I mentioned earlier, I recommend Dr. Dzung Vo's website https://mindfulnessforteens.com/guided-meditations. There's a 5-minute lovingkindness practice you can try.

Practicing Empathy

Empathy means "feeling with," truly understanding how someone else is feeling. I like to think of empathy as the first step toward compassion and kindness. It's a lot easier to be kind when we understand someone else's point of view and how he or she might be experiencing the world.

Danielle, who has cerebral palsy, realized that other kids teased her because they'd never gotten to know a person with a disability. She created a program for children with and without disabilities to participate in activities together. The kids had a great time, and they told her "how different it was to connect and build friendships with people with actual disabilities rather than just reading about them" (Dawson, E., 2018, p. 40).

Here are my favorite ways to practice empathy. The first focuses on people we know well, but maybe not as well as we think we do. The second practice focuses on people we think we don't have anything in common with, but maybe we're more similar than we realize.

Activity 38 will help you think about how we're all "Same-Same, But Different." I love this expression, which I learned from a family member who's done a lot of traveling in Asia. Your friends and family aren't exactly like you, and you can avoid a lot of stress and conflict if you think about how you're alike and how you may have very different perspectives and personalities.

Empathy doesn't mean we have to understand exactly what someone's life is like. We can never really get inside others' skin and experience the world the way they do. On the other hand, we all have the same types of feelings. Brené Brown (2018) said, "Empathy is connecting to the feeling under the experience, not the experience itself. If you've ever felt grief, disappointment, shame, fear, loneliness, or anger, you're qualified" to understand how someone might be suffering (p. 140).

I first practiced Activity 39: 1% Similar when I was in bed with the flu and the news was full of terrible stories of people suffering from Ebola. I realized that having the flu was maybe one hundredth, one thousandth, or even one millionth as bad as Ebola. It helped keep my own minor illness in perspective, and it also helped me to feel compassion for the victims and their families.

Ever since then, I think about how I'm "1% similar" to everyone in the world. Our culture, beliefs, or perspective may be different. There may be a lot that we disagree about, but we all have the same basic needs and feelings.

ACTIVITY 38
same-same, but different

Directions: Think about someone close to you, like your best friend or a member of your family. How are you same-same, and how are you different? You can write your answers in the space provided or in your journal.

1. What are at least two things you have in common? (For example, "we both have red hair," or "we both love old movies.")

   _____

   _____

   _____

2. What is at least one thing about you that's different? (For example, "I'm shy, but she's outgoing," or "I love figure skating, but she's into tennis.)

   _____

   _____

   _____

3. Based on these similarities and differences, what assumptions are you making about this person? Do you know that these assumptions are accurate?

   _____

   _____

   _____

4. How might you better support this person, in good times and bad, by trying to empathize with how he or she is actually feeling and what he or she actually needs?

   _____

   _____

   _____

Note. Adapted from "Two Powerful Empathy Practices to Awaken Compassion," by C. Hannay, 2019, retrieved from http://www.mindfulteachers.org/2019/06/two-empathy-practices.html. Copyright 2019 by C. Hannay. Adapted with permission.

ACTIVITY 39
1% similar: an empathy practice

Directions: Think of a person or group of people from a very different background than yours. Maybe it's hard to understand this person or group, or maybe you're in conflict with them. Can you think of any ways that you are actually similar to each other? Write about this person or people in your journal or in the space provided.

Name of Person or Group: _____

1. Why do I feel like we have nothing in common? _____

   _____

   _____

   _____

   _____

   _____

   _____

2. What are some ways we are actually similar? _____

   _____

   _____

   _____

   _____

   _____

   _____

This may be a tough activity, but it can be the first step toward solving a problem or conflict. A young man named Babatunde felt angry when he was threatened by a police officer. He found out there was a small group of police who were willing to talk with Black youth, and he was surprised to discover that these officers were just as concerned as he was about violence against young Black men. They helped Babatunde lead a series of training workshops for the police in their city (as cited in Dawson, E., 2018).

The situation didn't change overnight, and there are still a lot of major issues in his community, but Babatunde's story shows what can happen when people try to see a situation through each other's eyes.

Have you ever felt this sense of connection? Melissa Sutor had this feeling when her sister was diagnosed with cancer when they were both teens. At the hospital, it was the first time they were around a lot of kids from different backgrounds and with different religious beliefs:

> They were different, but it was so clear to me that we're all connected. That experience broke down a lot of barriers. It drove my curiosity about other beliefs. I wanted to understand other people and their experiences. That was life changing. (as cited in Dawson, V., 2018, p. 41)

If you try looking at things from someone else's point of view, you can always find a way that you're at least 1% similar. This can change the way you think about someone you don't understand, someone you find annoying, or even someone you dislike. Once you start looking for what you have in common, you may find that it's really more like 80% or 90% similar.

Father Greg Boyle (2017) has seen former members of rival gangs working together peacefully, once they get to know each other a little bit. They learn to say, "I know we're not friends, but let's not be enemies." Bugsy and Miguel used to be in rival gangs, so they hated each other. When they finally started talking, they discovered they had a lot in common. As Miguel put it, "I guess all I needed to do was meet his insides" (pp. 192–193).

It's important to acknowledge our differences, rather than assuming we share the same perspective. It's also important to acknowledge our similarities and connections, especially to people we might think are worlds apart from us.

In this chapter, we focused on being kind and extending good wishes to ourselves and other people, especially when they might be suffering. In Chapter 9, we'll focus on feeling grateful for all of the good people, things, and circumstances in our lives that we often take for granted.

an attitude of gratitude

As I mentioned in Chapter 2, we often take for granted the pleasant little moments we experience every day. That's too bad, because there are a lot of advantages to focusing on what we appreciate. Listing or writing about what you feel grateful for can help you sleep better and feel happier (Domet, 2018).

What do you feel grateful for right now? (See Activity 40: Gratitude for Everyday Things.) It doesn't have to be anything huge. You can pick some tiny little thing, like maybe the sun is shining or you're wearing your favorite pair of jeans.

Did it feel good to focus on something that you appreciate? How might it feel to try this every day? The gratitude journal is a popular way to make appreciation part of our daily routine. (See Activity 41: Gratitude Journal.) All you have to do is write down a few things, people, or circumstances that you like or enjoy or that helped you in some way.

Back in Chapter 1, I told you about how meditation teacher Melissa Sutor first learned about mindfulness from listening to the crickets and the birds with her grandma. Melissa's grandma also taught her about feeling

ACTIVITY 40
gratitude for everyday things

Directions: In the spaces provided or in your journal, write all of the things you feel grateful for right now. These can be people, places, pets, or plants—anything that makes you feel happier, healthier, or more comfortable.

1. _____

2. _____

3. _____

4. _____

5. _____

6. _____

7. _____

8. _____

9. _____

10. _____

ACTIVITY 41
gratitude journal

Directions: Each day this week, think about a few things that you appreciate. These could be actual things, like your favorite sneakers. Or they could be something that happened, or a place where you felt comfortable, or someone who was nice to you. Write about what you feel grateful for in the following chart or in your journal.

	I feel grateful for . . .	I feel grateful for . . .	I feel grateful for . . .
Sunday			
Monday			
Tuesday			
Wednesday			
Thursday			
Friday			
Saturday			

an attitude of gratitude

grateful: "Every morning, when she woke up, she would speak gratitude: 'Thank you, Jesus, for another beautiful day.' It didn't matter if it was storming or raining outside, she would give gratitude for the gift of another day" (as cited in Dawson, V., 2018, p. 41).

Beach volleyball player Kerri Walsh Jennings (2018) also likes to practice mindfulness and gratitude in nature. She said:

> I'm always bringing myself back to the moment by acknowledging the wind and paying attention to digging my feet in the sand. In the early morning on the beach, you can really feel the spirit of the world. That's what's so great about nature: You don't have to be rich to have the luxury of breathing it in. (para. 1)

Mindful Eating and Gratitude

How many times a day do you eat? How many times a day do you really focus on what you're eating? As I'm sure you've figured out by now, I think eating is a wonderful opportunity to practice mindfulness. In Chapter 2, you focused on the five senses while eating a snack. In Chapter 5, you focused on your bodily sensations, noticing when you feel hungry or full.

This time let's focus on appreciating what we eat. If you're like me and can easily go to a grocery store full of a huge variety of food, it's important not to take this abundance for granted.

Thich Nhat Hanh, a famous Vietnamese monk, liked to practice mindful eating by thinking about all of the different conditions that make our food possible. He said:

> A person who practices mindfulness can see things in a tangerine that others are unable to see . . . the tangerine tree, the tangerine blossoms in the spring, the sunlight and rain which nourished the tangerine. Looking deeply, one can see the ten thousand things which made the tangerine possible . . . and how all these things interact with each other. (as cited in Bays, 2011, p. 197)

Meena Srinivasan (2014) learned to eat mindfully at a talk by Nhat Hanh in New Delhi, the capital of India. The participants were each given a mosambi, a citrus fruit similar to an orange but with a green peel. As they slowly and mindfully enjoyed their fruit, Nhat Hanh asked them questions like "Where did this orange come from? How did it get here?" Srinivasan was amazed when she started thinking about the journey "from the seed to the soil to the farmers to the store that led to this sweet fruit on my tongue" (p. 46).

We don't have mosambis where I live, but I really enjoy citrus fruit. When I was growing up, my mom always put an orange in the foot of my Christmas stocking, even though it was easy to get oranges at the supermarket. That's because when she was a kid, Christmas was the only time all year she got to eat an orange, so it was very special.

I try to remember what a privilege it is to be able to eat fruit like oranges, tangerines, and grapefruit. They don't grow anywhere near where I live, so someone has to deliver them from hundreds, maybe thousands of miles away.

Your family may observe a period of fasting every year, like Yom Kippur or Ramadan. Or you may give up a favorite treat during Lent. All of these are good opportunities to appreciate food that you might take for granted the rest of the year. You can also try Activity 42: Mindful Eating Gratitude Practice and Activity 43: Say a Blessing Before Meals.

Be Grateful in All Things

I don't feel well today because I have a cold. Right now my throat is so sore that it's painful to swallow.

What a great time to practice gratitude!

Huh?

I can't say that I'm thrilled about having a cold. I'd much rather not have a cold. But as long as I do have a cold, I'm grateful to be safe and warm inside. And my husband went to the store to buy me soup and ice cream. So I'm grateful to him for doing that. I also appreciate how good they taste, and how they make my throat feel a little better.

At Thanksgiving dinner a few years ago, my uncle gave a blessing based on 1 Thessalonians 5:18 "Be grateful in all things." The idea is to be grateful IN all things, not necessarily FOR all things. This was quite a moving prayer, as it was such an awful time for our family—both my mother and my uncle himself were seriously ill. We weren't at all happy about the challenges we

ACTIVITY 42
mindful eating gratitude practice

Directions: Before eating a meal or snack today, think about all of the people who grew, transported, and prepared the food you're about to eat. Think about the sun and soil and seeds. If you're religious, think about how God provided this food for you to eat. In your journal or in the spaces below, write about the different people and circumstances that made it possible for you to enjoy this food.

I feel thankful for _____

_____

_____

I feel thankful for _____

_____

_____

I feel thankful for _____

_____

_____

I feel thankful for _____

_____

_____

I feel thankful for _____

_____

_____

Note. Adapted from "Three Ways to Practice Gratitude Every Day," by C. Hannay, 2019, retrieved from http://www.mindfulteachers.org/2019/06/three-gratitude-practices.html. Copyright 2019 by C. Hannay. Adapted with permission.

ACTIVITY 43
say a blessing before meals

Directions: Before every meal or snack today, take a moment to silently express appreciation for the food you're about to eat. If your family is religious, you may already say a prayer or blessing before meals. If you're not religious, you could think about the people who helped to make your meal possible, and send them good wishes and thanks for providing the food to you. In Japan, it's common to say *itadakimasu*, which translates to "I humbly receive."

You can write about your experience with blessings in your journal or by answering the questions below.

1. Does your family usually say a blessing before meals? Why or why not?

_____

_____

_____

_____

_____

2. What type of blessing feels most comfortable and authentic to you?

_____

_____

_____

_____

_____

3. How did it feel to give a silent blessing before every meal today? Would you like to try it again tomorrow? Why or why not?

_____

_____

_____

_____

_____

were facing, but we did feel tremendously grateful for the outpouring of love and support from our friends and neighbors.

Can you think of any ways to be grateful during challenging times? Write about them in your journal or in Activity 44: Be Grateful in All Things.

Appreciating What You Take for Granted

As I mentioned in Chapter 5, a lot of teen girls are very critical of their bodies and any perceived flaws they might have. Could you try focusing on what you appreciate about your body instead? Do you ever think about how amazing it is that your body can do so many different things so easily?

Imagine what it would be like if we had to tell our tongues what to do: "Move part of that bite to the right side. Look out! Here come the teeth, get out of the way! Time to swallow—no, wait! Not when I'm breathing in!" (Bays, 2011, p. 181). Try using your nondominant hand to do things like brushing your teeth or eating a meal. (If you're right-handed, use your left hand, and if you're left-handed, use your right hand.) This can help you to appreciate all of the things your body can do. It can also help you feel compassion for people who may not be able to do these types of daily tasks, perhaps because they've been injured or have a medical condition that affects their movement (Bays, 2011).

Dena Simmons (as cited in Dawson, 2019) has a twin sister with a chronic illness. She said:

> Every single day I have the privilege of waking up without pain. My sister does not. I pray every day, asking for her not to suffer. Sometimes, the privilege we forget about is our ability to not feel pain in our body. (p. 38)

My colleague Brandi Lust leads workshops on mindfulness, gratitude, growth, and connection. She likes to practice gratitude by thinking about the people who don't have access to all of the privileges she takes for granted, like running water. She shares her thoughts in Activity 45: Appreciating What I Take for Granted.

In this chapter we focused on appreciating all of the good things in our lives. In Chapter 10, you'll learn about how you can use your gifts and advantages to help other people.

ACTIVITY 44
be grateful in all things

Directions: In the chart below, I've given a few examples from my own life. Can you fill in the rest of the chart with examples from your life? We all have big and small problems to deal with. You can choose any experience that you didn't want to happen but that helped you learned something.

Something Bad That Happened	Why I Feel Grateful
Example: I have a sore throat.	My husband went to the store to buy juice and cough drops and soup and ice cream. The soup and ice cream taste good.
Example: My car broke down.	I wasn't injured; several people helped me.
Example: My mom got cancer.	Our extended family, friends, and neighbors were very kind; I became closer to my sister; I learned how to help people when a family member is sick.

ACTIVITY 45
appreciating what i take for granted

Connecting with others' suffering is a way to cultivate profound gratitude for what you have. This is different than feeling guilty. Instead, it's about being deeply, profoundly appreciative. I have sometimes struggled with the guilt I feel for my great fortune. However, I try to remember that recognizing and appreciating my many gifts is also honoring those who go without.

For example, I could take for granted the running water and indoor plumbing in my home, accept it as a given and barely even notice it's there; this is a perspective of great privilege.

Or, I can remember that having drinkable water is a luxury. I can remind myself of the incredible convenience and pleasure of not having to go outside in the middle of the night to use the restroom. This is a much humbler perspective that also pays homage to others less fortunate.

Appreciating What You Take for Granted

Directions: Choose a daily experience that's important to you, and try to imagine your life without it. As you do this, think about people in the world who are living in the situation you are imagining. Then, over the next 24 hours, notice when you are reaping the benefits of this gift, and give thanks.

The gift you choose to appreciate in this way could be a physical convenience like indoor plumbing, running water, food, clothing, access to information, or medical care. However, you could also choose to direct your awareness to the psychological resources many go without: comfort from loved ones, belief in yourself, or trusting relationships with your friends and family.

Each time you are reminded of this gift, spend a moment to silently give thanks for being the recipient. Notice how this changes your experience. Then, at the end of the day, spend some time reflecting on how your life would be different if you didn't have this element of your life permanently.

1. Which "gift" did you choose to appreciate today? _____

_____

_____

_____

_____

_____

_____

2. How would your life be different without it? _____

_____

_____

_____

_____

_____

_____

3. Did your perspective change while doing this activity? Why or why not? _____

_____

_____

_____

_____

_____

_____

Note. Adapted from *Myths of Being Human: Four Paths to Connect with What Matters*, by B. Lust, 2018. Copyright 2018 by B. Lust. Adapted with permission.

sharing your gifts with the world

A long time before the Internet, there was Indra's Net, an ancient Hindu teaching about a limitless web connecting every life to all other lives. At every little knot in the net, there's a jewel that represents one life. Each jewel reflects all of the other jewels in the net, meaning that each individual life reflects all other lives (Srinivasan, 2014).

Many cultures have an image of the interconnectedness of all life. Most Native American tribes have a word that translates as "All My Relations," which refers to our interconnection with each other and with all of nature (Evans, 2018).

Haitians say "Nou spagheti." We're inseparable, like strands of spaghetti woven together (Magloire, 2013). In Zulu, there's a similar concept called Ubuntu:

> When we want to give high praise to someone we say, "Yu, u nobunto"; "Hey, so-and-so has ubuntu." It means "You are generous, you are hospitable, you are friendly and caring and compassionate. You share what you have. It is to

say, "My humanity is inextricably bound up in yours." We belong in a bundle of life. (Archbishop Desmond Tutu, as cited in Torgovnick, 2013, para. 6)

How are you connected? Who do you feel connected to? How can you nurture connections with others? In your journal or in Activity 46, write or draw "My Web of Connections."

If you truly appreciate how interconnected we all are, it can help you be more generous in sharing your time and resources with people in need. As Oprah Winfrey (2019) said:

Notice where there is a need, then do whatever you can to help . . . It takes only one candle to light a whole room of darkness. People think, Oh, I have no power to change the world. But . . . how you treat every person in your world has an impact . . . Don't underestimate your power. Hate is potent, but so is kindness. And goodness, and grace. Use yours generously. (p. 100)

I felt very sad when I read that only 20% of high school students and 30% of college students "feel they live purposeful lives" (Mindful, 2018b, p. 16). Activities 47–49 will help you figure out how to bring more kindness to the people in your own little corner of the world, which is the first step toward making your own unique contribution to the world at large.

Activities 50 and 51 will help you think about the people you admire, either real people or your favorite characters from books and movies. Why do you admire them? How can you be more like them, not just in the future but starting today?

One of my biggest role models is Rosa Parks. I doubt she ever heard the word *mindfulness*, and it's unlikely that she ever practiced the specific techniques I've described in this book, but I still consider her a model of mindful speech and compassionate action.

As I'm sure you know, Rosa Parks is famous for the day when she refused to give up her seat on a racially-segregated bus in Montgomery, AL. She was angry about being treated like a second-class citizen, but she was able to remain calm and treat other people respectfully.

You may not know that Parks also helped her community in a lot of other ways. To give just one example, after her neighbors' house was

ACTIVITY 46
my web of connections

Directions: In the space below or in your journal, write a description or draw a picture or diagram of your "web of connections" to the people in your family, your community, and the world. If you tend to be critical of your own writing or drawing, remember that this is just an exercise. You don't have to show it to anyone else if you don't want to.

sharing your gifts with the world

ACTIVITY 47
the gift of your presence

Directions: Think of someone who'd appreciate your time and attention, and spend a while hanging out with this person. It could be a new kid at school, or it could be someone who's much younger or older than you, like your little cousin or your grandpa. After you do this, answer the questions in the spaces provided or in your journal.

1. Who did you give the gift of your attention? _____

_____

_____

_____

_____

_____

2. What happened? How did he or she respond? _____

_____

_____

_____

_____

_____

3. Would you like to try this again, with the same person or a different person? Why or why not?

_____

_____

_____

_____

_____

_____

ACTIVITY 48
my week of kindness

Directions: Every day this week find someone who could use your help. Then, write about your experiences in the chart below or in your journal.

Acts of Kindness		
	Who Did I Help?	What Did I Do?
Sunday		
Monday		
Tuesday		
Wednesday		
Thursday		
Friday		
Saturday		

1. How did it feel to do a small (or big) act of kindness every day? _____

_____

_____

2. Would you like to try this again next week? Why or why not? _____

_____

_____

sharing your gifts with the world

ACTIVITY 49
give a sincere compliment

Gratitude and compassion are sometimes described as *complementary practices*, which means that they go together really well with mindfulness. The first time I heard this, I misunderstood and thought the person was talking about complimentary practices, like paying compliments. I actually think that's a really good idea, so let's try a "complementary complimentary" practice. (Can you tell that I used to be an English teacher?)

Paying compliments is one way to be kind to the people you know, as long as the compliment is sincere. A lot of times girls will give each other a fake compliment. They might do this to make fun of another girl or because they want something from her. Other times, girls might compliment somebody they like because they're flirting. Not that you can't flirt if you want to, but this is different.

You could:

- tell your favorite teacher something you like about his or her class,
- tell your parents or caregivers that dinner was really good tonight,
- tell your best friend that she looks nice today, or
- tell your little sister she did a great job on a drawing.

Directions: Give someone a compliment today, then write about your experience in the spaces provided or in your journal.

1. Who did you compliment? _____

_____

_____

_____

_____

_____

2. What did you say? _____

_____

_____

_____

_____

_____

being you   120

3. How did the person react?_____

_____

_____

_____

_____

_____

4. Would you like to keep giving people compliments?_____

_____

_____

_____

_____

_____

5. Why or why not? _____

_____

_____

_____

_____

_____

ACTIVITY 50
who are my role models?

Directions: Think about the women or men you most admire, and answer the questions below. You can write your responses in your journal or in the spaces provided.

Your role models could be fictional characters, like Hermione Granger from the Harry Potter series, or they could be real people like Emma Watson, who played Hermione in the films. Did you know that Emma Watson is not only an actress and an advocate for women's rights, but also a qualified yoga teacher?

You don't have to be exactly like your role model. Nobody is exactly like anybody else. But you can use this person's example to inspire you and help you think about what you'd like to do in the future. You can also think about what kind of role model you'd like to be right now in your daily life.

Name of Role Model #1: _____

1. Why do I admire this person? _____

_____

_____

2. How could I become more like this person in the future? _____

_____

_____

3. What can I do right now in my current life to be more like this person? _____

_____

_____

_____

Name of Role Model #2: _____

1. Why do I admire this person? _____

_____

_____

2. How could I become more like this person in the future? _____

_____

_____

3. What can I do right now in my current life to be more like this person? _____

_____

_____

_____

Name of Role Model #3: _____

1. Why do I admire this person? _____

_____

_____

2. How could I become more like this person in the future? _____

_____

_____

3. What can I do right now in my current life to be more like this person? _____

_____

_____

_____

ACTIVITY 51
mindful or mindless characters

Directions: Think about one of your favorite books or movies. How do the characters show, or not show, mindfulness and compassion? For example, in *Little Women*, Jo's not paying attention so she accidentally burns Meg's hair and cuts Amy's foot. And there's an example of kindness and compassion when the sisters decide to give their delicious Christmas dinner to a family that needs it more than they do.

You can answer the following questions in the spaces provided or in your journal.

Present-Moment Awareness

1. Is there a time when a character fully realizes and appreciates what's happening in the present moment? What happens?

_____

_____

_____

2. Is there a time when a character is *not* aware of the present moment? What happens?

_____

_____

_____

Mindful Speech

1. Is there a time when a character says something true, helpful, and kind? What does he or she say? How does it affect the other characters?

_____

_____

_____

2. Is there a time when a character says something untrue, unhelpful, and/or unkind? What does he or she say? How does it affect the other characters?

_____

_____

_____

Kindness and Compassion

1. Is there a time when a character shows kindness and compassion toward another person or animal? What does he or she do? How does it affect the other characters?

_____

_____

_____

2. Is there a time when a character does *not* show kindness or compassion toward another person or animal? What does he or she do? How does it affect the other characters?

_____

_____

_____

What Would You Do?

1. If you were a character in this story, what (if anything) would you do differently? Why?

_____

_____

_____

Note. Adapted from "Mindful or Mindless? Analyzing Characters in Books and Movies," by C. Hannay, 2015, retrieved from http://www.mindfulteachers.org/2015/12/mindful-or-mindless-characters.html. Copyright 2015 by C. Hannay. Adapted with permission.

bombed, she quietly went into the kitchen and swept up the broken china. Then she helped buy them a new set of dishes (Hudson & Houston, 2002).

In both her public and private actions, Parks was dealing not just with broken dishes but with a broken world.

It might feel overwhelming to face the problems in the world, but there is always something you can do to help. I've had a lot of conversations with my sister, Pastor Deb, about the importance of mindfulness and compassion. I really like what she said in one of her sermons about how every small gesture or action makes a difference (Sunoo, 2018):

> Something that's been coming up in conversation with my rabbi friends recently is the Jewish concept of *tikkun olam*, which in English simply means repairing (or mending) the world. *Tikkun*, the verb for "repair," is the same verb used in modern Hebrew for fixing a broken bicycle, repairing a computer that's stopped functioning, or mending a torn shirt.
>
> I wonder how many situations in which we currently feel overwhelmed could actually be reconsidered from the perspective of: "OK, but where is my part? What could I fix here? What's mine to repair?" Let's find ways to pick up our tool kits and get to work, repairing the world one small break, tear, knot, or scrape at a time.

The Civil Rights Movement wasn't just a couple of actions by famous individuals like Parks and Dr. Martin Luther King, Jr.: "It was hundreds of thousands of people, often young people, deciding they were going to be different—kinder, braver, more inclusive, through small choices made each and every day" (Dawson, E., 2018, p. 5).

As this book comes to a close, think about what you hope to accomplish in your life, and what kind of person you'd like to be. You can write about this in your journal or in the spaces provided in Activity 52: My Interests, Goals, and Aspirations.

While reading this book and doing the activities, you've learned how to be more present in your life and more compassionate toward yourself and other people. You can see just how much you've learned by taking Quiz #2: How Much Do I Know About Mindfulness? and comparing your answers to the quiz you took in the introduction.

I wish you all the best as you continue Being You.

ACTIVITY 52
my interests, goals, and aspirations

Directions: In the space provided or in your journal, write about what you want to do in the future and who you want to be.

1. What are my interests? *(What do I want to explore and learn?)* _____

_____

_____

_____

_____

_____

_____

2. What are my goals? *(What do I want to achieve and accomplish?)*_____

_____

_____

_____

_____

_____

_____

3. What are my aspirations? *(What kind of person do I want to be?)*_____

_____

_____

_____

_____

_____

_____

QUIZ #2
how much do i know about mindfulness?

Directions: Circle the answer that shows how much you agree with each statement, from "not at all" (0%) to "definitely" (100%).

1. I understand clearly what mindfulness is and how it can help me.

   not at all   not really   a little bit   sort of   definitely

2. I pay attention to my surroundings and to what I'm eating.

   not at all   not really   a little bit   sort of   definitely

3. I always understand exactly how I'm feeling, and I never get overwhelmed by my emotions.

   not at all   not really   a little bit   sort of   definitely

4. I understand how the brain works and how it can be affected by mindfulness practice.

   not at all   not really   a little bit   sort of   definitely

5. I know several different types of breathing practices for mindfulness or relaxation.

   not at all   not really   a little bit   sort of   definitely

6. I know several different types of body-based practices for mindfulness or relaxation.

   not at all   not really   a little bit   sort of   definitely

7. I never feel stressed when I'm trying to communicate with my friends, family, and teachers.

   not at all   not really   a little bit   sort of   definitely

8. I always find it very easy to treat myself and other people with kindness and compassion.

   not at all   not really   a little bit   sort of   definitely

9. Every day, I express appreciation for the good things in my life.

   not at all   not really   a little bit   sort of   definitely

10. I often share my gifts, advantages, and resources with people in need.

    not at all   not really   a little bit   sort of   definitely

It's fine if you didn't answer "definitely" to all of the questions. If you answered "not really" or "not at all," just go back and reread those chapters and try the activities again. Remember what I keep saying: Mindfulness is a practice, not a perfect. Be very gentle with yourself as you gradually keep increasing your awareness.

references

Allan, B. (2015). *How teachers can share mindfulness with their students* [Web log post]. Retrieved from http://www.mindfulteachers.org/2015/11/how-teachers-can-share-mindfulness.html

Bartolomeo, J., Furlong, E., & Handa, J. (2018, Oct./Nov.). Perfectly me! *Seventeen, 77,* 78–83.

Bays, J. C. (2011). *How to train a wild elephant and other adventures in mindfulness.* Boulder, CO: Shambala.

Beck, M. (2001). *Finding your own north star: Claiming the life you were meant to live.* New York, NY: Crown.

Bernstein, J. (2017). *Mindfulness for teen worry: Quick and easy strategies to let go of anxiety, worry, and stress.* Oakland, CA: Instant Help Books.

Boyce, B. (2018). The magnificent, mysterious, wild, connected and interconnected brain. *Mindful.* Retrieved from https://www.mindful.org/the-magnificent-mysterious-wild-connected-and-interconnected-brain

Boyle, G. (2017). *Barking to the choir: The power of radical kinship.* New York, NY: Simon & Schuster.

Brown, B. (2018). *Dare to lead: Brave work. Tough conversations. Whole hearts.* New York, NY: Random House.

Bullock, B. G. (2018). Mindful research news: More kindness, less judgment. *Mindful.* Retrieved from https://www.mindful.org/mindful-research-news-more-kindness-less-judgment

Dahl, M. (2018). *Cringeworthy: A theory of awkwardness.* New York, NY: Portfolio/Penguin.

Dawson, E. (2018). *Putting peace first: 7 commitments to change the world.* New York, NY: Viking.

Dawson, V. (2018). Charting her own path. *Mindful, 6*(3), 38–43.

Dawson, V. (2019). Coming full circle. *Mindful, 7*(1), 36–38.

Domet, S. (2018). The power of thanks. *Mindful, 6*(5), 18–19.

Dweck, C. (2006). *Mindset: The new psychology of success.* New York, NY: Ballantine Books.

Engeln, R. (2018). The surprising downside of Instagram compliments. *Psychology Today.* Retrieved at https://www.psychologytoday.com/us/blog/beauty-sick/201811/the-surprising-downside-instagram-compli ments

Evans, K. (2018). To speak the truth: Mindfulness in the Native American tradition. *Mindful, 5*(6), 52–57.

Feldman, L. (2018). How teens are redefining the conversation around depression, according to actor Rowan Blanchard. *Time.* Retrieved from http://time.com/5278452/rowan-blanchard-mental-health

Fonseca, C. (2017). *Letting go: A girl's guide to breaking free of stress and anxiety.* Waco, TX: Prufrock Press.

Gelb, M. J. (2004). *How to think like Leonardo da Vinci: Seven steps to genius every day.* New York, NY: Dell.

Gilbert, P., & Choden, P. (2014). *Mindful compassion: How the science of compassion can help you understand your emotions, live in the present, and connect deeply with others.* Oakland, CA: New Harbinger.

Hannay, C. (2014a). *Noticing the five senses: A daily mindfulness log* [Web log post]. Retrieved from http://www.mindfulteachers.org/2014/12/five-senses-mindfulness-log.html

Hannay, C. (2014b). *Rainbow walk: A mindfulness activity to move the body and rest the mind* [Web log post]. Retrieved from http://www.mindful teachers.org/2014/10/rainbow-walk-mindfulness-activity.html

Hannay, C. (2015a). *Counting sounds: A mindful walking practice* [Web log post]. Retrieved from http://www.mindfulteachers.org/2015/03/counting-sounds-mindful-walking-practice.html

Hannay, C. (2015b). *Five senses snack: A mindful eating chart* [Web log post]. Retrieved from http://www.mindfulteachers.org/2015/08/five-senses-snack-mindful-eating-chart.html

Hannay, C. (2015c). *Mindful or mindless? Analyzing characters in books and movies* [Web log post]. Retrieved from http://www.mindfulteachers. org/2015/12/mindful-or-mindless-characters.html

Hannay, C. (2015d). *Next time, I'll do better: Recognizing and learning from mistakes* [Web log post]. Retrieved from http://www.mindfulteachers. org/2015/03/next-time-ill-do-better.html

Hannay, C. (2015e). *T.H.I.N.K. before you speak: Case studies in mindful speech* [Web log post]. Retrieved from http://www.mindfulteachers. org/2015/04/THINK-before-you-speak.html

Hannay, C. (2016a). *Five contemplative art practices* [Web log post]. Retrieved from http://www.mindfulteachers.org/2016/08/contempla tive-art-practice.html

Hannay, C. (2016b). *T.H.I.N.K. before you speak 2: Case studies in mindful speech* [Web log post]. Retrieved from http://www.mindfulteachers. org/2016/01/think-before-you-speak-2.html

Hannay, C. (2019a). *Count the ways to count the breath* [Web log post]. Retrieved from http://www.mindfulteachers.org/2019/05/count-breath.html

Hannay, C. (2019b). *Four more ways to focus on the five senses* [Web log post]. Retrieved from http://www.mindfulteachers.org/2019/05/five-more-five-senses.html

Hannay, C. (2019c). *Mindful speech: What type of conversation do you want?* [Web log post]. Retrieved from http://www.mindfulteachers. org/2019/06/mindful-conversation.html

Hannay, C. (2019d). *Three ways to practice gratitude every day* [Web log post]. Retrieved from http://www.mindfulteachers.org/2019/06/three-gratitude-practices.html

Hannay, C. (2019e). *Two powerful empathy practices to awaken compassion* [Web log post]. Retrieved from http://www.mindfulteachers. org/2019/06/two-empathy-practices.html

Headlee, C. (2017). *We need to talk: How to have conversations that matter.* New York, NY: Harper Wave.

Heller, R. (2015). *Secular meditation: 32 practices for cultivating inner peace, compassion, and joy.* Novato, CA: New World Library.

Himelstein, S. (2019). *Trauma-informed mindfulness for teens: A guide for mental health professionals.* New York, NY: Norton.

Hogan, K. (2018, October-November). Nude awakening. *Seventeen, 77,* 54–55.

Hudson, R. (Producer), & Houston, R. (Director). (2002). *Mighty times: The legacy of Rosa Parks* [Motion picture]. United States: Tell the Truth Pictures.

Jennings, K. (2018). How Kerri Walsh Jennings is using volleyball to start a mindfulness movement. *Shape.* Retrieved from https://www.shape.com/celebrities/interviews/kerri-walsh-jennings-beach-volleyball-mindfulness-movement

Levy, R. (2014). *Celebrating the ordinary women of STEM* [Web log post]. Retrieved from http://www.mindfulteachers.org/2014/03/celebrating-ordinary-women-of-stem.html

Lust, B. (2018). *Myths of being human: Four paths to connect with what matters.* Author.

Magloire, B. (2013). *Work of the heart, for the heart, and for the people of Haiti* [Web log post]. Retrieved from http://www.mindfulteachers.org/2013/07/work-of-heart-for-heart-and-for-people.html

McAneney, C. (2016). *I have been cyberbullied. Now what?* New York, NY: Rosen.

Mindful. (2018a). Open your mind, learn something new. *Mindful, 6*(4), 12.

Mindful. (2018b). Top of mind. *Mindful, 6*(1), 12–16.

Mosley, R. (2018, Aug./Sep.). How Sabrina rolls. *Seventeen, 77,* 78–85.

Nardo, D. (2017). *Teens and eating disorders.* San Diego, CA: Reference Point Press.

Neff, K., & Germer, C. (2018). *The mindful self-compassion workbook: A proven way to accept yourself, build inner strength, and thrive.* New York, NY: Guilford Press.

Paulsen, B. (2019). Tap into your inner brilliance. *Mindful.* Retrieved from https://www.mindful.org/tap-into-your-inner-brilliance/

Popowitz, C. (2017). *Grief recovery for teens: Letting go of painful emotions with body-based practices.* Oakland, CA: Instant Help.

Rabois, I. (2016). *Compassionate critical thinking: How mindfulness, creativity, empathy, and socratic questioning can transform teaching.* Lanham, MD: Rowman & Littlefield.

Rabois, I. (2018a). *Mindful listening in a noisy world* [Web log post]. Retrieved from http://www.mindfulteachers.org/2018/08/mindful-listening-noisy-world.html

Rabois, I. (2018b). *Mindful cell phone use, for students and teachers* [Web log post]. Retrieved from http://www.mindfulteachers.org/2018/09/mindful-cell-phone-use.html

Rabois, I. (2019). *Befriending yourself and creating a mindful learning community* [Web log post]. Retrieved from http://www.mindfulteachers. org/2019/03/befriending.html

Rathbone, B., & Baron, J. (2015). *What works with teens: A professional's guide to engaging authentically with adolescents to achieve lasting change.* Oakland, CA: New Harbinger.

Reilly, P. (2015). *A path with heart: The inner journey to teaching mastery.* Tompkins Cove, NY: Irimi Horizons.

Ricci, M. C. (2018). *Nothing you can't do!: The secret power of growth mindsets.* Waco, TX: Prufrock Press.

Saltzman, A. (2018). *A still quiet place for athletes: Mindfulness skills for achieving peak performance and finding flow in sports and life.* Oakland, CA: New Harbinger.

SARK. (2000). *Transformation soup: Healing for the splendidly imperfect.* New York, NY: Simon & Schuster.

Smookler, E. (2019). The good news about being wrong. *Mindful, 6*(6), 30–32.

Snyder-Roche, S. (2017). *Calming young minds* [Web log post]. Retrieved from http://www.mindfulteachers.org/2017/08/calming-young-minds-interview.html

Srinivasan, M. (2014). *Teach, breathe, learn: Mindfulness in and out of the classroom.* Berkeley, CA: Parallax Press.

Stanley, A. (2018, Aug./Sep.). Do you have streak stress? *Seventeen, 77,* 68–69.

Sunoo, D. (2018). *Repairing the world.* [Web log post]. Retrieved from http://www.magpres.org/sermons/repairing-the-world-isaiah-586-12-and-micah-66-8

Telgemeier, R. (2010). *Smile.* New York, NY: Graphix.

Torgovnick, K. (2013). *I am, because of you: Further reading on Ubuntu* [Web log post]. Retrieved from https://blog.ted.com/further-reading-on-ubuntu

Twenge, J. M. (2017). Have smartphones destroyed a generation? *The Atlantic.* Retrieved from https://www.theatlantic.com/magazine/archive/2017/09/has-the-smartphone-destroyed-a-generation/534198

Vo, D. (2015). *The mindful teen: Powerful skills to help you handle stress one moment at a time.* Oakland, CA: Instant Help.

Walsh, K. (2019). Research news. *Mindful, 7*(1), 12–13.

Weis, S. (2017). *The top three breathing exercises for anxious kids* [Web log post]. Retrieved from http://www.mindfulteachers.org/2017/08/breathing-for-anxious-kids.html

Werker, K. (2014). *Make it mighty ugly: Exercises and advice for getting unstuck even when it ain't pretty.* Seattle, WA: Sasquatch Books.

Winfrey, O. (2019, Jan.). What I know for sure. *Oprah, 20*(1), 100.

Wiseman, R. (2002). *Queen bees and wannabes: Helping your daughter survive cliques, gossip, boyfriends, and other realities of adolescence.* New York, NY: Three Rivers Press.

about the author

Catharine Hannay is a writer and teacher. She publishes the website Mindful Teachers (http://www.mindfulteachers.org) and is a regular contributor to the Center for Adolescent Studies blog.

Catharine studied literature in college, and she has master's degrees in teaching and communications. She can speak French and Spanish, and she has a strong interest in other languages and cultures. She's taught students from all over the world, and she spent a year studying in Paris and 18 months working in Osaka, Japan.

You can learn more at http://www.catharinehannay.com.